PR

THE CENTERED LIFE

The Centered Life gives the road map and tools to answer 3 major life questions we all ponder. Where do you want to go? What do you want to do? Who do you want to be? Imagine how different your life would be if you could answer these questions—only then will you understand the divine gift Esther Jones-Alley has given to all who will open the pages of this awesome, easy to read book. It will change your life forever!

~**Dr. K. Mhina Entrantt,** author of *What Grandma Knew about the Law of Attraction*

Each time I am in the presence of Coach Esther, my sister, my friend, and always my coach, I am reminded of the journey to enjoy the physical presence. Learning how to have appreciation and gratitude for the only thing that living truly offers–a physical experience, has become the reminder of the gift of life that I learned from her. I am ecstatic that the world can now be witness to her very special wisdom and embrace a journey of love, respect, self-worth, and greater humanity.

~**Vivian Phillips,** Seattle-area Arts and Cultural Leader

THE
CENTERED
LIFE

THE CENTERED LIFE

A SPIRITUAL LIFE
COACHING JOURNEY

ESTHER   JONES-ALLEY

Made for Success
PUBLISHING

Made For Success Publishing
P.O. Box 1775 Issaquah, WA 98027
www.MadeForSuccessPublishing.com

Distributed by Made For Success Publishing

First Printing

Library of Congress Cataloging-in-Publication data

Jones-Alley, Esther
  The Centered Life: A Spiritual Life Coaching Journey
    p. cm.

      ISBN: 9781613398371
      LCCN: 2015915959

Printed in the United States of America

For further information contact Made For Success Publishing
+14255266480 or email service@madeforsuccess.net

DEDICATION

I would like to dedicate this book to my mother, Dorothy Nadine Jones, (1925-2001) because without her I would not be here. She gave me life; I am her seventh child out of nine, her largest baby weighing in at 11 pounds, 8 oz. and she allowed me to come through her. She nourished me even though she had eight other children, she taught me and gave me my sense of belonging in a family. She gave me my values, my foundation and courage to go out into the world and be the best I could be. She loved me even when I wasn't lovable. She loved every one of her children, from the oldest to the youngest. She held her brood together in her loving arms, she sacrificed with grace to raise her children by faith, she loved one and all she held them deep within her heart's wall. Her strength, wisdom and patience were unmatched and her commitment to her nine children was unwavering.

I also want to dedicate this book to Bishop John Ernest Holmes, my first spiritual teacher. He was the first person to tell me that I had a choice whether I lived or died and that I could speak directly to the Universe/God. I watched him grow and evolve into one of the highest Avatars I ever had the opportunity to be in the presence of and experience spiritual teaching. Because of him I embarked upon my spiritual path rather than languishing in religion.

CONTENTS

FOREWORD

here are people we meet in life that serve a moment and others a lifetime. Often those people are invisible to us, never receiving acknowledgment or full understanding of the positive influence and impact on the way we see and make meaning of our lives. Literature, poetry, dance, music and all forms of human expression that touch our hearts, still our soul and compel our bodies to engage life represent a spiritual act, one that reminds us of how important it is to be ordinary while experiencing the extraordinary condition of being a human.

These ideas I am sharing are not mine alone, they are reflections I have received personally from professional coaches around the world. 70% of the countries in the world enjoy a community of professional coach practitioners. Coaching is both a capacity and a vocation defined by our global standards body, the International Coach Federation, as a partnership that offers a thought-provoking and creative process that inspires people to maximize personal and professional potential. Our Author, Esther Jones-Alley is a proud ICF Credentialed Member, well trained and deeply committed to the evidence-based practice of coaching that is transforming lives and society.

Esther is a person, a fully alive, centered and joyous being, that touched me more than a decade ago, offering her authentic self and dramatically diverse experience with generosity, respect and a little bit of sass. To be in the presence of another who chooses to live fully present, centered and available for whatever life presents, that's wondrous and priceless. I am honored to offer a peak into the journey you will enjoy reading this book and learning about your own wondrous, priceless life that unfolds, by your choice, when living a centered life as the spiritual discipline you pursue. You will also recognize the remarkable resource available through engaging with a professional coach, in this case a coach who focuses on your Spiritual Life as the pathway to centered, fulfilled living.

As a young girl I was curious about God, who was he, or was he a she, or what exactly was God since I couldn't see him or her or truly know whether the prayers I was encouraged to speak each morning and night were ever heard by anybody but me! Evidence of God in my life came quickly when I was out in Nature and, not so much when around adults who seemed to think my view of the world was "childish and fantasy." Of course I obeyed and as life now passes into decade six, each day delivers an experience of pure spiritual bliss on this planet and all the miracles that living here on Earth provides. I feel lucky and privileged to live at a time when choosing to be awake and present to my life and the community I invite each day is celebrated. This is not always so in human society. For far too many of us the denial of human love and joy continues in this world.

I believe deeply in the power of human connection that allows for respectful sharing, questions and choices. A relationship with a professional coach offers a resource for choosing wisely and respectfully no matter what our life circumstances may be. Are you wondering how to get started? Maybe you wonder if you are ready? What do you notice yourself saying inside about choosing a coach? This book will answer these questions and more as you step onto the path and engage with a Spiritual Life Coach. You will begin right where you are. The ingredients for living an authentic, satisfying, fulfilled life are already inside of you, patiently waiting for you to choose to unleash your unique energy, passion and love in the world.

People will often ask me the question, "My life is terrific, why do I need a coach?" Perhaps you perceive the underlying assumptions in the question such as coaching is about fixing problems and need is about weakness. My reply usually sounds something like this, "What do imagine is the next possibility you want for your life and what will support you to choose to pursue that dream now?" Partnering with a professional coach offers a safe environment for self-reflection and self-awareness so we remember what matters most. When that clarity arises, we also access our inspiration and alignment with the core of who we are. Alignment creates ease to tap into our courage and internal gifts and resources so that we risk a new choice. Choices are presented everyday that stretch us beyond our habits and auto-pilot navigation of life in order to engage in ways that generate progress toward a goal or dream we want to fulfill. We do have everything inside to be the author of our lives, beyond the circumstances that can feel daunting; we restore our integrity and response-agility individually, with our families, our communities and society as a whole. This is a state of being that every person may choose in every moment, to be sovereign.

As you read through the steps of the journey that is available when partnered with a professional coach, this book offers beautiful pearls that reflect Esther's life path such as Estherisms and poetry that her soul channels for all of us to appreciate. There is no replacement for wisdom that generates from life experience. Seeing all experiences as a whole, without partition, denial or rejection, all are threads in the tapestry of life that reflects our unique beauty. Being with a coach offers the opportunity to reclaim our magnificence and this book will reveal the step-by-step journey of an enriching coach partnership.

Life is a path, one that requires tending, by you and only you in order to live a centered life that honors the gift of being alive. What fulfills your destiny and how does being centered ensure your success? Having a companion on that path that accepts responsibility for being curious on your behalf so that you truly see your authentic self and fully embody your wholeness. This foundation is the beginning of building a new house inside your life that is a safe harbor for all that you dream – that is the experience of coaching that reading this book offers. You will laugh, cry, relate, forgive, chose again and transform because you will imagine the life you always wanted and see it manifest in small steps along the way.

I am both grateful and proud of Esther and know that through your reading you will make a new friend for a lifetime.

~Janet M. Harvey, ICF Master Certified Coach
inviteCHANGE CEO &
Managing Director of Talent Solutions
International Coach Federation Global Past President
International Coach Federation Foundation President

INTRODUCTION

The year was 1973 and I was exploring the world around me, enjoying my newfound freedom and living my life in a manner that was totally different from the way I was raised. My sister and I were living fast and hard; we had every recreational drug available to us whenever and wherever we wanted them. We smoked a joint to get our day started, and the weekends were filled with a myriad of drugs; uppers and downers, whatever it took to keep us going. The freezer always had five or six hits of coke, and we kept a shoe box of weed in the cabinet of the living room table along with all of the weed paraphernalia. Bennies (uppers) were given to me by the jarful. We both worked very hard and played even harder. I was in my early twenties and a single mother of a three-year-old daughter (Ieshia). My sister had no children and no plans to have one anytime soon. We were feeling a new kind of freedom and great distance from the very large, deeply religious, constricted family we were born into. We had escaped the small-town drudgery of Monrovia, where we grew up and moved on to the big city, the bright lights and a smorgasbord of new adventures in Long Beach.

My sister worked at a fish cannery in San Pedro while I held down a job in a local lamp factory. We weren't making a lot of money, but for that time it was enough for us to live on and have some fun on. We enjoyed the basic necessities and some extras, like my shoe collection and my brand new bright yellow Volkswagen bug with the Rolls Royce front end. Wow, I thought I was hot stuff. I enjoyed the fact that it was a four speed, because if I was high, shifting the gears would keep me alert, and there were more nights than I care to remember that the shifting worked and got me home safely. The phrase "Living for the weekend" became our motto. We worked all week just so we could party all weekend. I always had two or three wigs ready to wear, and my platforms were always in style and ready for dancing. We would start getting ready about 6 p.m. on Friday night – make-up was put on with meticulous artistry and utmost care. Most of the time something new and brightly colored that revealed lots of skin in all the right places covered my tall, slim, but curvy body. Hot pants were really in and combining them with a mid-drift top was the norm, or maybe just a hot pant jumpsuit would do the trick. I would finish off the look with a pair of the latest platform shoes and by 9:30 p.m. I was ready for the first leg of the weekend.

My running partner was another young mother named Hilary. Hilary had three small children and her family lived nearby, so she always had a built-in babysitter. My sister didn't always run with us; she had several partners she ran with, but a lot of the time we all ended up together at the latest hotspots in LA. Most clubs closed at 2 a.m. but there was always the after-hours clubs that didn't close until 6 or 7 a.m. and of course we had to have breakfast at the local Denny's, which meant we didn't get home most times until 9 or 10 a.m. This was our lifestyle and we were totally immersed in this lifestyle. If we weren't at the clubs, we'd be at some hip house party of one of my sister's friends from the cannery, or a concert of whatever artist was in town. My sister and I had gotten completely away from our roots; the strict religious upbringing that was devoid of the recreational drugs, alcohol, cigarettes and partying of our new world.

Rewind about five or six months earlier; our mother sent word that our bishop wanted my sister and me to come to church. He wanted to talk to us about our lifestyle, so off we went to visit church. Three of my brothers at three different times had also visited us and told us to move out of Long Beach and come home prior to my mother's invitation from the Bishop. So we agreed to go and see what the big deal was. We went to church, great service, but we didn't really know what was going on, we were just there, being obedient. So right after church we stopped to talk to the Bishop as he requested; he always had some tid-bits of wisdom to share or some future prophecy to look forward to. I jumped in front of my sister because I wanted to be the one to sit closest to the Bishop in hopes that he would share some special prophecy with me, something that would uplift my life, for in my heart I knew my life was totally out of control. The Bishop gasped when I sat down, and said, "You just took her place". I had no idea at that time what he was talking about, but I was surely going to find out.

Bishop Holmes was a soft spoken man and he often spoke in parables when giving a message, but this time he was very straightforward and told us we needed to change our wicked ways and rein ourselves in, for if we didn't we would surely perish. He told us about a spiritual experience in which he stepped into a star trying to save the life of a woman named Sis McMillan. She was new to the church, and her son had tried to kill her and had succeeded in killing her mother—his grandmother—and leaving his mother, Sis McMillan, in a coma. He told us after reaching Sis McMillan and rescuing her spirit, how on his way back from this experience he saw my sister and me, and as he tried to get to us, a lamb got between him and us and he couldn't reach us. Now at the time this meant nothing to me. I didn't understand any of it and thought, what has that to do with me? I knew it was some kind of a warning, some kind of message, but I didn't understand it. If my sister understood at the time she didn't let on. The Bishop asked us to slow down and to come and visit the church more often. So we left that meeting promising to return to church and to change our wicked ways, but we didn't. I knew I was young, healthy, good-looking, and made to party, so I figured I had time to come back into the fold, but it wasn't going to be right away. I knew that then was not the time; I was having too much fun.

We went right back to our life as if nothing had been said; I continued to work at the lamp factory during the week and partied the weekends away. Then one morning I got up feeling sick to my stomach. I didn't think much of it, I just thought I had partied too hard, and I would stay home and rest – things would be better tomorrow. How wrong I was. I got sicker and sicker. I was in such pain I went to the emergency room, but they couldn't find anything wrong, so they gave me some antacids and sent me home. I made that trip to the emergency room several more times, hoping to get some relief. Sometimes my sister was right there with me, other times I drove myself to the hospital. I went again and again, but they couldn't find anything wrong with me. I kept going to emergency because I didn't have a general practitioner at the time; sickness was not a part of my lifestyle hence no need for a doctor. I was so sick I couldn't hold any food down; I threw up everything I ate. They would give me something to settle my stomach at the hospital and something for the pain, but no answers. I was truly scared; I knew I was really, really sick. I had lost so much weight that my bones were visible through my clothing. I could see and count every rib, and I could see the outline of my pelvic bones. I looked like a skeleton. Still no answer from the emergency room visits.

I had been absent from work for about three weeks and I felt like I needed to go back. Once my bowels moved, I started to feel a little better, although still very weak but at least I wasn't throwing up anymore. So I showed up to my factory job on that Monday morning bright and early, but something was terribly wrong. Everyone I passed seemed to have this strange look on his or her face as they stared at me. My supervisor came up to me and asked me to come into her office. Her face went pale and she was visibly shaken. She looked at me and told me to get to my doctor immediately, and have them test me for Yellow Jaundice or hepatitis because I was yellow and looked like walking death. I started to cry, hearing her words; I was just so tired and scared. I told her I had been back and forth to the hospital and got no answers, but at that moment in my supervisor's office I felt a bit of relief. I had something to go on, like I had finally gotten some answers. She told me she couldn't allow me to stay at work because I was really sick and needed to get to my doctor. I could be contagious and she couldn't allow me to infect the rest of the workers.

I got into my yellow VW bug that matched my yellow skin and eyes, and drove straight to my gynecologist office, since that was the only doctor I had a relationship with on a regular basis. Once I arrived I asked if they would do a blood test on me for Yellow Jaundice or Hepatitis. The nurse took one look at me and sent me to the lab to have blood drawn. She told the lab to rush the testing, and to immediately send the results to the doctor. She told me to come back to their office so the doctor could see me with the results. My gynecologist confirmed it – Hepatitis. He gave me the name of a local Internist to make an appointment for treatment. I was no longer afraid I was numb and resigned.

I remember thinking I was going to probably die because another girl that grew up with us (Brenda Ward) had just died of hepatitis. I didn't know anything about this disease nor had I heard of it until Brenda died from it. She was so pretty and so young, with everything to live for, just like me--at least the young part. She left behind a little girl just as I was going to have to do – too many similarities. I felt a strange calmness; I was resigned to my fate.

I went back to my apartment and gave my sister the bad news; she seemed to take it in her stride. She hadn't even really noticed that I'd turned yellow until I showed her the inside of my mouth and told her to look into my eyes—where they used to be white they were now yellow. I turned over my hands and made her look; my palms were yellow, in fact all of my skin had a yellow hue. My sister was quite confident that if I went to the doctor, he would fix me right up and everything would be back to normal. I didn't share with her how I felt in my heart about what was happening to me. So I made the appointment and went to the Internist. He gave me his plan for treatment, which consisted of plenty of rest and a bland diet. He told me my liver was very sick and would have to heal itself, and there was no medicine they could give me to help the healing process. Needless to say, what he told me didn't change how I felt about my fate. I went home, got into my bed and tried to rest. My little girl was only three and she needed some attention through all of this, so my rest was not as ample as it probably should have been. My sister helped out when she got home from work but she was still getting high and was kind of spaced out about the whole thing.

That night after going to the doctor and getting my treatment plan, I was lying in my bed. It was completely dark in my room, my daughter was already asleep in her crib, and I had just dozed off to sleep myself. I was woken by a voice calling my name. The voice was very clear and loud – Esther. It frightened me. I sat straight up in my bed and as my eyes adjusted to the dark I looked around my room to see if anyone was there, but there was no one; at least no one I could see with my natural eye. But I knew, I knew in my heart that Death had called. I was at rock bottom, I had nowhere else to go and death had come to lay claim on my soul. (In hindsight I now know it was a call to life. It was the beginning of my awakening. It was actually the Angel of Life).

I got up and went to my sister's room and told her what had happened. She barely woke up, and she seemed lost in her world of marijuana and sleep. I was too afraid to get back in my bed, so I went into the living room and fell asleep on the couch. From that night on I never slept in my bed again but I knew it didn't make any difference. Death had made himself known and I needed to get my house in order; moving from the bed to the couch would not stop Death. I needed to make sure my child would be taken care of once I was gone and that my affairs were in order.

I decided to make my rounds to all of my family members and old friends in my hometown. I had the overwhelming desire to visit as many people from my past as I could and I knew my time was running out. I wanted to see them all one more time before I died, and that is truly what I felt in my heart. I was weak, but I wasn't in pain anymore so I could drive myself around to take care of my business. I had to make sure my little girl had clothes and shoes to last for a while. I had to make sure my car insurance was paid and the car would be paid off. Once I was gone, I didn't want my child or my death to be a burden on my family. My life insurance was paid up and my job still had me on payroll, so financially things would be fine.

I made my rounds to all of my old friends, and the response was the same from all of them: "Oh my God, what's wrong with you?"

My final stop was my mother's house and I felt the need to talk very seriously with my younger sister about her and her husband mooching off my mom; she was not amused to say the least. She was offended and went crying to my mom in great protest, of course twisting my words so they seemed like daggers in her heart. My mom immediately jumped to the defense of my sister (her usual position) and admonished me for getting into their business. The arrangement they had was just fine with her (their company more than made up for the financial cost to my mom. I didn't understand then, but my mother needed to be needed regardless what the cost). I tried to defend myself and explain that I was only trying to give some advice one last time because I could see the damage it was doing to both parties involved. But my mom raged on and of course I would not relinquish my position because I could see things in a more heightened consciousness at this point in my journey.

My mother became so angry she reared back to slap me. Suddenly she stopped; all of the blood drained from her face and tears streamed down her pale cheeks. She turned away and cried out loud. (My mother had the sight. She came from a long line of seers; she had the gift of prophecy).

"What's wrong?" I asked, over and over again.

My sisters came running into the kitchen where we were, asking, "Madea, what's wrong? Why are you crying like that?"

She finally composed herself enough to speak. "All I saw was blood when I went to hit Esther. All I could see was blood. She is dying. Oh my God, she is dying."

I stood there with tears rolling down my face, already aware of the knowledge of my pending death. She came back over to me and put her arms around me, still crying and trembling. "I'm sorry, I'm sorry," she said as she ushered me to the couch.

I told them I had made this trip to say goodbye. My mother cried harder as I tried to explain what I knew to be true of my situation.

"Have you gone to the doctor? What did the doctor say?" she asked through her tears.

I told her, yes, I had been to the doctor and he told me to get plenty of rest and eat a bland diet, and that the liver had to heal itself. I tried to end the conversation as quickly as possible. I was tired, I didn't want to talk about it anymore and I had a long drive ahead of me. I knew there was nothing they could do for me and it was apparent that my words of deathbed wisdom had no effect on my younger sister. They were now caught up in the drama of my illness for which they couldn't do anything but cry and ask me questions I couldn't answer.

I went back to my apartment in Long Beach and took my place on the couch, resigned to my fate. My sister returned to her life of going to work and coming home and getting high; she was not connected to the seriousness of the situation. I told my sister I wanted to go to church that Sunday and I wanted her to go with me. She wasn't too keen on that idea but agreed to go with me; she could see I was getting weaker. Sunday morning came and I was up early since I wasn't really getting much sleep anyway. I woke my sister up to her dismay, since she was getting high until late in the night, and then I got my daughter up and dressed. Somehow we were able to get it together enough to get on the freeway headed to Monrovia. When we got to the church the service was in full swing so we tried to find seats as quickly as possible.

The spirit energy was high in the service; people were up singing, clapping and praising God, and everyone was having a joyous time. The mood seemed to change once we were seated for a few minutes. Things began to die down, people sat down and the spirit began to cool. The Bishop got up and walked across the church; he didn't say anything, but he began to sing a slow song. That was his way of bringing the spirit to another level; slower, but higher, more controlled.

I knew his next move. I knew he would start reading people he was going to prophesy and I knew I would not be spared. As the song was caught up and carried on by the congregation, he told my sister and me to stand up. As we stood there it seemed like an eternity; all eyes were on us. I could see my mother and grandmother crying. Many of the other church saints were crying too, but I didn't cry. I was resigned. I was prepared to make that transition from the body to the spirit. Bishop Holmes looked at me and turned his head away and began to weep out loud. When he turned back he said, "Little girl, I see your death certificate. It has been signed." At that moment, it seemed like the whole church started to howl and cry aloud. Bishop went on, "Your sister is going to lose her mind once you are gone. She will no longer be in this world (he was speaking of her mental state). I have prayed and I have requested prayer from the Great Fathers, the Kahunas, and they have sent back word that they can't intercede."

My sister and I just stood there, no tears, no expression and no words uttered. Bishop went on but I couldn't really hear anymore. I was numb, spaced out, no longer in that place. The Bishop, this holy man who had been my hope, my rock throughout life had just sealed the deal with his prophecy. The next thing I remember, someone was tugging at my arm to sit down. I don't remember much else about that service, but at the end, when everyone shook hands and said their goodbyes, I went to shake Bishop's hand, thank him, and say goodbye. Bishop looked at me and said, "If you want to live and make it through this, you will have to go to God for yourself. You will have to make the connection. No one else can do it for you. You can live if you choose to."

Those words scared me more than anything he had said to me that day.

His words, "You can choose" were like a foreign language to me. He was saying that God would hear me, although I didn't quite understand at the time. I was scared because I had relied on my mother and grandmother to get a prayer through for me. Whenever I was in trouble, I would always call on them to get a prayer to God for me, but now The Bishop was telling me I had to do this for myself. How was I supposed to go about this? My very life depended on it and I had no clue how to pray.

We went back to our apartment in Long Beach, my sister and I, and before the week was out, my brother Gideon came to see us and told us he was there to take us back home. My mother wanted me to be there with her and Bishop had said it was time for us to leave Long Beach. We had to leave now. Well, I was too weak to protest and my sister agreed reluctantly, but said she would stay behind to pack up our things. Gideon would not go back without me, so I had to get things together for me and my little girl, knowing I might never see my things again, and most certainly I would never see my apartment again. Three of my other brothers went later on in the week to help my sister move all of our things back home.

Once we got to my mother's house, she immediately started fussing over me, and she had already prepared a bed for me in her living room, since all of the bedrooms were already occupied with my baby sister and her kids. It didn't matter, I just wanted to sleep, and I was at peace with the world and myself. Mildred, my sister-in-law, had taken Ieshia to her house to stay so I didn't have to worry about her. As I lay there on the opened couch in my mother's house, I had no worries and no cares. When I closed my eyes all I could see was this bright white nothingness; everything was pure white, a white I had never seen before. I spent most of the next day sleeping off and on, when suddenly there was a loud knock at the front door. Madea hurried to the door to open it because she didn't want me to awaken. Too late, my peace was disturbed. It was my oldest brother,

Ernest. He was crying so hard she could hardly understand what he was trying to tell her. She let him in, and told him to calm down so she could understand him. He slowed down and took a deep breath. He said, "Bishop said to get Esther to the hospital now. She is lying there dying. We have to take her there now, Madea, now."

I was too far-gone to care about what he was saying. Things moved in slow motion for me now. Next thing I knew I was in the back seat of someone's car and we were on the freeway. I remember being put into an examining room at the hospital. There was a foul smell in the air; someone near me had defecated on himself or herself, but I couldn't focus on that. The doctor came in and examined me but said nothing to me. I heard him ask who was there with me and my mother and the whole clan stepped forward. I heard the doctor tell my mother, "Lady, if you know how to pray, you better pray, because there is nothing that I can do for her. She is in the third stage of the disease and it is in God's hands now".

I heard the cries and screams as they went up from my family but it really didn't faze me. All I wanted to do was sleep.

I spent the next three days in quarantine, mostly sleeping. The only time I was awake was when my mother came and woke me to try and get me to eat. She came every day and just sat by my bed and prayed. She would wake me to feed me and clean me up and I would tell her my dreams.

I asked her about things when I was a baby because I had just dreamed it. She was my only connection on this side of consciousness--she represented life. After a few days they moved me to John Hopkins Liver Hospital because there was nothing else that could be done for me at that hospital, and at Hopkins they specialized in liver diseases.

I continued to have the dreams, vivid dreams, and my mother was always there to hear them and to confirm the events I saw. It was as if my life was replaying through my dreams. For fourteen days I laid in that hospital with no change to my condition. The poison still flowed through my system, my liver was swollen and I hadn't gained back one of the many pounds I'd lost. Daily they drew blood, looking for a change, hoping for the healing process to kick in, but nothing -- there was no change. Finally my doctor decided he needed to do a liver biopsy to see why my liver was not healing. Well, I knew what that was about because I'd heard other patients on my floor talking about it and I was not going to have anything to do with a liver biopsy. I was scared; I didn't want them sticking a huge needle in my back while I lay perfectly still as they pulled a piece of my liver out to examine. I wanted nothing to do with that; nothing. The biopsy was scheduled, but somehow I knew deep within my soul that I would not have the procedure. I don't know how I knew, but I knew.

That night, I was getting ready to go to my dream world as usual. I went to the restroom and I was humming a hymn. I can't remember the name of the hymn; I just know it was soothing to my soul. I felt spiritually lifted for the first time since becoming ill. I went to bed and for the first time I didn't dream, in fact I can't remember anything of that night.

MY AWAKENING

When I rose the next morning I could see the light coming through the corner windows in my room. I jumped out of bed and went to the window; I saw the sun as if for the first time. I could see the tops of the trees and it was as if I had never seen a tree before, but intellectually I knew what it was, the same with the grass and the flowers. I knew somewhere deep within my soul that I was healed; I was going to live. I didn't understand why I saw the world as I did, but I was seeing the world through new eyes, and in my mind it was as if I was looking back at someone else's life and memories. I was in that body, but it really wasn't mine and this wasn't my life. I felt brand new and I was drawing from the memory bank of this person who once possessed this body I now occupied. I was a watcher, I could tap into any part of Esther's life and instantly learn what I needed to know, and it was strange; very strange.

When the phlebotomist came to draw my blood, I told him emphatically I was going home today. He looked at me and replied, "I don't think so. You have to get better first."

"I am better," I shot back at him. "I'm fine now. I'm all better now and I'm going home."

I went to the phone and called my mother and told her I was coming home today. She was shocked to say the least, but she tried to calm me down and said she would be there soon. When the doctor came in for his morning visit I told him I wanted to go home. I was all better and I wanted to go home today. He looked at me in amazement since I was so adamant about going home, and he said if the bile count went down and I gained five pounds he would let me go home tomorrow. In his own way he was blowing me off; he didn't really expect me to go home, he was planning a biopsy. That sounded like a fair deal to me so I agreed and calmed down for in my heart I knew it would be so. I knew I would get out of that hospital the next day. All the rest of that day I grew stronger and stronger and I continued to get comfortable with my new surroundings. I could see more and I understood more; a fire burned in my soul. That night I did dream, but I don't really remember it as I had on previous nights, I just knew I did.

The next day when the phlebotomist came in to draw blood, I felt excited. I wanted to know the results right away, but he told me I would have to wait until my doctor came in to see me. I had already weighed myself and I could hardly wait for the doctor. I was ready to go home. When the doctor came he was surprised that my bile count had gone back to normal and I had gained five pounds as well. He said he had never seen anything like it before. Not since becoming a doctor had anything like this ever happened to any of his patients. Needless to say I went home that day, back to my mother's house. It was a little strange at first, but I was able to draw on the memories enough to be comfortable. Everyone said I was different. I looked different and I talked different; I felt there was a new peace about me. I knew I had a new lease on life and I was going to take full advantage of it. I had a brand new thirst to know everything I could about God, the Universe and the goodness therein. I wanted to study and read everything I could get my hands on about man's relationship to that Universal power known as God. This was the beginning of my spiritual journey, the beginning of my walk to a greater understanding of my purpose. I knew I had a reason for being here and from this point on I would do whatever it took to understand that reason.

It would be more than thirty years before I fully embraced the emergence of the gifts that came from that experience. The spiritual awakening had begun and as I moved forward along my journey, it led me to the work I do today. Because of this experience, I have become more aware and tuned in to others' spirits, allowing me to support the people I serve. With finely tuned sensibilities I will encourage you to go deeper within for answers to your pressing issues.

Through divine wisdom and practical applications I will encourage you to co-create the most authentic life possible. The events that took place so many, many years ago have allowed me to be the Spiritual Life Coach I am today.

1

SETTING THE AGENDA

o you've decided to hire a coach. The first step for you to get started is to figure out your agenda. Before we get into that, let me share a bit about how I realized the importance of the agenda. I remember when I first realized I had been coaching most of my adult life but didn't know that's what it was called. I just knew that what I was doing was a calling for me. It was what made my heart sing.

People showed up in my life with a multitude of issues and problems. It didn't matter whether the problem was as personal as a break-up, a divorce or a new love relationship. Sometimes it was a problem with a new supervisor or the fear of testing for a promotion. It didn't matter what it was, I saw them all and I engaged in solving whatever issue was at hand. I enjoyed my coaching work more than the job I was being paid to do. My job was easy and boring; I could do it with my eyes closed. I was so content when doing the work with others that I knew in my heart I was not in sync with my soul's mission. Looking back over the years of working in a corporate environment, I always had someone at my desk telling me his or her problems. At the time, I didn't have any formal training as a coach and I didn't know the method of a professional coaching process. I believe when I started my journey of working with others, coaching had not yet become an actual profession. It was many years later and after years of experience at working through people's issues that I learned about the profession of life coaching.

A NEW CAREER WAS LOOMING

When the concept of life coaching was first introduced to me, I thought, *that's what I've already been doing for so many years;* I just didn't have the formal training. After doing some investigation into the requirements and training necessary to get certified I knew this was just another path on my journey. It took me a few more years before I began that leg of my journey, but once I began, I was completely immersed in the training and soaked up everything I could about the coaching process. As I began to learn and grasp this new concept I could see how the work I had been doing differed and what steps were missing from the way I had been working with people. I became aware of a coherent set of codes, rules and processes that comprised this profession. It was organized, learnable and doable, one just needed to commit to studying and learning when and how to apply this knowledge. It was a system that was designed to support, ask questions and get results, always moving the client forward. One of the most important steps I learned about that had been missing when I was working with people was the very first step: Setting the Agenda.

SOME BACKGROUND FOR SETTING YOUR AGENDA

Now you may say, "Agenda? What agenda?" Well, everyone has an agenda in life; what's yours? I didn't ask that question years ago while working with my friends and co-workers. I didn't know to ask nor did I know how important setting an agenda was to the success of getting to the end results. I didn't have the skillset to do the work as effectively as I should have; I was missing the roadmap. I was able to support most everyone that showed up at my desk, just not at the level I could have if we had the roadmap. What it would have taken to help them years ago is virtually the same knowledge that is necessary today. Asking the correct questions and understanding that there are a few rules such as respecting the other person's boundaries and privacy goes a long way in this process.

LET THE JOURNEY BEGIN

Let's begin the journey. Setting the agenda for the work that must be done together takes up a good deal of the first session. It is crucial that in this session the guidelines, boundaries and a level of working trust are established.

You will probably have some type of tool that will be the basis of your work of setting the agenda. Most coaches use worksheets, personality tests or other tools to help you get started. Make no mistake; a lot of work will happen in this session. This meeting will cause you to pull from the depths of your being to access the issues to put together and shape a working, living, fluid, and flexible roadmap.

All of the business and technical components of the coaching relationship are completed within this initial meeting as well. There is nothing more important in this process for both of you than setting the agenda.

In order to develop your agenda, a working relationship must be established. The three elements that encompass this relationship are:

> *Trust*
> *Respect*
> *Freedom of Expression*

All three must be mutual. The agenda is the roadmap and shows both of you which way to go, at least in the beginning. Also, it is a living, fluid and flexible roadmap, therefore the agenda can definitely change and take on a different form once this journey has been embarked upon, just as the relationship will change too.

THE ELEMENT OF TRUST

A working trust is the minimum that must be established between both parties. Trust means different things to different people and the onus of quickly developing an environment of trust falls squarely on the shoulders of your coach. Yet in order to create this environment of trust, both of you must be open and willing to step out in faith and believe this very new relationship is safe, will work, and will continue to grow.

The promise to be a good listener and ask relevant questions to help you get to clarity should come from the coach. This is not something that can be faked or glossed over. Both parties must discuss it openly and honestly within the first thirty minutes of the session, although it will take longer than thirty minutes to conclude. The coach can be very conscientious, skillful and sincere and still fail to establish this bond.

It may take a little more time and interaction with each other before you are comfortable enough to open up to begin to trust. It's paramount to the success of this relationship that you both get to that place of trust. If you don't feel safe enough or comfortable enough in this session then you will not share honestly and you will not be open, making it a very unproductive session. If that's the case in this first meeting then this may also be a sign that this coach is not a good match for you.

What does trust really mean in your coaching relationship?

Trust is a belief that someone or something is reliable, good, honest, effective, and authentic. When you meet someone you believe is trustworthy, this means you have discovered you can take action based on his or her word. You feel secure that they will maintain your confidences and that you can depend on them to do what they say they will do.

What does the opposite of trust look like?

You also may have encountered untrustworthy people at the other end of the spectrum who have lied to you, cheated you, betrayed you, and have not been supportive of you. There are always two sides to life; we live in a world of duality and both types of people exist in our world but there is no place in the coaching relationship for the latter type of person. Neither one of you can afford to show up as an untrustworthy person if the coaching relationship is to be successful.

How do we build trust?

To build trust you must start the relationship as you intend for it to go forward. If you want to know the end, look at the beginning because the relationship will end as it began when it comes to trust. Once a high level of trust is established, it is easy for the coach to motivate you and

Setting The Agenda

for you to be motivated. If your confidence in the coach is high then you feel safe sharing your feelings and thoughts because you know the environment is safe and secure. The relationship is healthy, collaboration thrives, and results increase.

Estherism: Follow the Behavior

I have these sayings I call "Estherisms." They are my guiding principles and values. One of my Estherisms that pertain to trust is, "Follow the behavior". It means that a person can tell you anything, but if you really want to know what that person is truly all about then you must watch what they do; follow their behavior. This has helped me to see if I could or could not trust a person when they wanted my trust.

THE ELEMENT OF RESPECT

Respect is the second element of building the relationship to set your agenda. In order to get respect you must be willing to give respect. Respect must be demonstrated between both parties in this first meeting if the conversation is to proceed. Without respect you will not trust the coach to listen to you honestly and sincerely. Also, you will not feel comfortable sharing your innermost thoughts and feelings in that environment.

43

What is respect?

Respect is having a high or special regard for the other person. It is holding someone in highest esteem and giving special or particular attention to that person whenever you are in his or her presence. I'm sure we all have had the opportunity to experience some level of respect whether it was giving it or receiving it. I believe one must be willing to give respect in order to get respect because it is not always given to you first. The art of respectful listening to you is a key element that helps to begin the process of building a working trust. And respectful listening to you by the coach will also cause you to be willing to listen in return.

Respect or trust?

Respect is a different kind of trust. The kind of trust that determines whether people want to interact with you or not; talk to you, spend time with you or open up and share their feelings with you. Being respectful draws people to you that'll want to be around you, they'll tell their friends about you and they'll want to be in a relationship with you. Respect is a mutual contribution that is exchanged between you and the coach. Respect for each other's autonomy and choices ensures that you have full participation in generating solutions and strategies for issues on your agenda. Respect and trust go hand in hand in building the coaching relationship; there is no opposition between the two, they are one in the same. You can't have trust without respect, nor can you have respect without trust.

THE ELEMENT OF FREEDOM OF EXPRESSION

Without the freedom of expression, you as a client cannot ignite your passion, stir the excitement within you, and your drive to find your way to a more authentic life is dead.

Why is freedom of expression so essential in the coaching process?

This element of the coaching relationship allows both parties to explore their honesty and allows the light of truth to shine from deep within. Freedom of expression allows everything to come alive in the present moment for you. Even though nothing is certain and possibilities are endless within the coaching relationship, without the freedom of expression, your conduits of creation stop flowing and eventually shut down. In the process of setting the agenda both parties must flow in the element of freedom of expression to move beyond the illusory vices that hold them back from creating an agenda full of passion.

Last but not least.

Freedom of expression may be the last of the three elements but it is no less important than the other two. In the coaching relationship it allows you to be yourself without judgment, inhibition, criticism or constraint. You have the opportunity to speak your truth just as you see and understand it and the coach is there to support you every step of the way. Freedom of expression takes away the fear of what others may think or say about you and allows you to be your unique and most authentic self.

WHERE DO YOU WANT TO GO?

The most important question to answer.

Where do you want to go? It's the coach's duty to support you in becoming clear on this point and working with you to set a clear and workable agenda. This question may not be answerable by you at first. This process can be very difficult for you as it is for many other people, but don't fret; most people don't know where they want to go yet. Sometimes they're not clear about what they want and when they want it. Your coach will work with you to bring some clarity to this question. Even if you come into the process with your agenda in written form, this question still may not be answered for you. All of us have our own unique path and it's at this point in the process that you will be seeking to find your path.

It's not just a simple question.

This question, "Where do you want to go?" may seem like a simple one but there is more to it than meets the eye and there may not be a quick answer. I have presented this question many times during my coaching career and each time the answer is different and many times disjointed. The answers could range from you wanting a new job, to finding a new partner or finding more cohesion within your family unit, to getting in touch with your inner self. You may be focused on the destination, which is never really that relevant -- it's always about your journey. The growth and the experiences that will be gained on your journey will far outweigh the arrival. You may find that what is believed to be your stated destination is not at all where you really want to go and is just the beginning of the next journey. "It's the journey not the destination" has been my favorite quote for as long as I can remember. I use it as part of my signature and my website because I know that the richness and the essence of your life will be found on the journey.

Estherism: It's Never a Done Deal

Just when you think you have arrived or you have completed the lesson, you may have just begun a new journey. We are spiritual beings having a physical experience. We are here to remember who we are and each of the experiences we have are created and called forth by our higher selves to assist us. We draw people, situations and places into our immediate consciousness to help us to continue our growth toward remembering. When you stop learning, experiencing and growing you become stagnant and die. Think about it; a pond must have an inlet and an outlet or the water just sits there and begins to smell as it stagnates.

LARRY AND THE LIFE STAR EXERCISE

The Life Star is a tool and exercise I use to help clients get clear on where things are in their life. The star has eight points, each one representing a different area of life, and the client rates each area using a percentage of 0 up to 100% as to how satisfied they are with that area of their life. This exercise helps us to identify the most critical area in their life and gives them the opportunity to prioritize which areas they want to begin their work. I'd like to share a story here with you about a former client and his Life Star exercise. I'll call him Larry, to protect his privacy.

When we started the exercise, I asked Larry where he wanted to go. His response was, "I need help with getting my business off the ground." He said all other areas of his life were in order. He had a wife who he loved very much and two children he was very proud of. His in-laws were great and his extended family was too. He said that financially he was doing just fine. So he felt that a few sessions should help him to arrive at his destination. As we began setting his agenda, his focal point was to develop some strategies to advance and expand his business in the most efficient manner.

Once we started his journey, somewhere in the second month Larry showed up to his session showing signs of stress and distraction. So after some well placed questions about his progress on his agenda,

Larry decided he wanted the session to take a more personal tone. He was having some issues with his wife and they were not in agreement about how to discipline the children. Here is where his agenda changed direction and we began another journey to address those issues, which then brought forth some deeper issues involving his in-laws and his finances.

Larry's case is pretty typical of the clients who seek out coaching. Their agendas are often multi-layered but they are not aware of that at the onset of the coaching relationship. That's why I said at the beginning of this chapter that the agenda is the roadmap and more than likely will change once you embark on the journey. The client's agenda changes along with where they want to go as the coaching sessions progress.

The agenda is a working, living, flexible document. It is fluid and as you move along your journey you must be open and accepting of the evolution of your coaching relationship. What is key here is that you always have full control of your agenda. The coach is there for support and to hold you accountable. Many things will shift and change; as issues are resolved, new issues can and will surface on the path to get where you want to go.

TYING IT ALL TOGETHER

Setting the agenda is the first and most crucial step in the coaching process. It is the roadmap and tells both parties where you want to go. This step must be completed if the coaching relationship is to thrive and if your goals are to be realized. This has always been a stimulating, exciting and thought provoking stage of the coaching process to me. This can be a delicate time and a time of bonding, and your coach must be committed to ensure a smooth and successful first step. Both of you will encounter surprises, and delights, and momentary bliss as you get a glimpse into the many opportunities and possibilities that life has to offer you.

The task of setting the agenda becomes a very doable mission when all three elements are in place and you have completed the exercises. You can move forward and develop a working roadmap that encompasses your goals and dreams. With everything in place both parties can move forward and begin to figure out where you want to go. Now let's get moving forward to the next step on this journey.

2

ESTABLISHING A TIMELINE

*H*ow fast or slow the coaching process goes is up to you. Establishing a timeline is the next critical step after setting the agenda. The timeline will help to hold you accountable to yourself and your coach. You can setup individual timelines for each issue or project you choose to work on, or you can just set up one overall timeline to determine the duration you want to work with the coach. Timelines are usually associated with goal setting because a timeline will help you to stay focused and help you to know where you are at any point in the process. This is the accountability phase of the coaching process. Although the coach is there to support and hold the space for you, they will also hold you accountable by reminding you of your timeline and the things you have set forth to accomplish.

YOU MUST BE WILLING TO INVEST

This is your life, your future, so you must be willing to invest in it. The concept of self-investment may be new to you, but it is necessary for your success. You must be willing to spend the time, energy and resources on yourself first. Oftentimes you are so willing to give to everyone else until nothing is left for you. You give up your time for work and career, your energy to children and spouses, and your resources to family and friends, only to find there's nothing left for yourself. Sometimes you give and give until there is hardly anything left to run your own systems. This is most unfortunate because the sad thing is, most of the time you are not even aware of the fact that you're running on empty. Sometimes you don't realize there is nothing left to give to anyone else until it's too late and your systems shut down either physically, mentally and/or emotionally. Sometimes you also become spiritually depleted, and once you are running on empty spiritually, that's when your life is at a critical stage. When you deplete yourself to this point, the soul is hurting and needs immediate attention. Investing in yourself is the only way to move forward along your timeline. Investing in you is the best move you can make as you travel the path to self-fulfillment.

Estherism: You Can't Give What You Don't Have

You may think you can, and that you must solve all of the world's issues, or at least all of your family problems. You can't fix everything; even if that everything is not yours to fix, you try to fix it anyhow. You don't even realize that you don't have it to give, and you don't even know that you don't always have to have it to give, so you try, and eventually you cry. The key is to first acknowledge that. The way for you to acknowledge that is by stopping, getting still, and listening to your spirit. You spirit will let you know that, "You can't give what you don't have".

COMMITMENT

Commitment is required on your part if you are going to set and reach your goals. You must be willing to commit to believing, trusting and supporting yourself first. The coach is there to hold the space and to hold you accountable to that commitment but you must do the work. There may be times when you find that time seems to be passing but you're not moving, and you never seem to know where it goes. Commitment is what it takes to transform the promises you make to yourself into the reality you so desperately want. Commitment is the glue that holds your promises, dreams and desires together until you transform them into your most authentic reality. When you are committed you will make better decisions and you will be willing to do the research to get more information before making those decisions. When challenges arise along the way it is commitment that will give you the strength and courage to persevere and continue moving towards your goals. Commitment to oneself doesn't mean you become rigid and inflexible; it means you must be willing to approach your goals with everything you've got—in other words, wholeheartedly.

You may feel that even though you are truly committed to yourself and have set up a timeline to work on your individual issues, you just don't have enough time to get everything done. In that case you may decide you want to optimize your schedule and at this point the coach may suggest you consider keeping a time log. By keeping a time log for a week or two you can monitor how and where you spend your time. A little time is involved in keeping a time log. It involves recording how you spend your time every minute of the day but the benefits are well worth it. (See the example at the end of this chapter.)

PUTTING IN THE WORK

You have decided to invest in yourself and you are committed to the process. Now the work begins to put a timeline together that is workable for you. Goals are good tools that can be set up and scheduled at this point. Your goals can pertain to any part of your life and address any issue you choose to face. Whatever you decide to work on at this stage can become a goal.

There are very specific steps to goal-setting, and many different techniques. One of the most commonly used techniques, SMART, is attributed to Peter Drucker's management by objective concept. **SMART** is a mnemonic acronym. Each letter stands for a step in the goal-setting process. I will explain below:

SPECIFIC – specific means stating your goal clearly, exactly and precisely. Here is an example of a non-specific goal: "I will make more cold calls". A specific goal is: "I will make ten cold calls five days a week for a total of fifty calls per week".

MEASURABLE – measurable means including clear criteria to measure your progress. In the above specific goal, the number of cold calls (ten), the number of days (five), and the total of calls per week (fifty) are criteria that can be measured. It also tells you what duration of time the calls will be made.

ATTAINABLE – attainable means to reach an end result, or to come into passion of, or obtain. So your goal must be something you can obtain, something you can reach. Maybe in your business making ten calls a day for five days a week is not something you can truly do starting out. You may want to set a goal for three calls a day and work your way up to ten after you become more proficient at making calls. When you identify goals that are important to you then you will begin to figure out ways to attain them. You will do what is necessary, like learning a new skill, changing your attitude and outlook and increasing your abilities. The attainability of the goal will tell you what it takes to complete your goal. Remember you must not set a goal that is too far out to reach or that you see as impossible because you will neither commit nor stay with it for the long term.

RELEVANT – relevant means your goal must be realistic, but still push you toward growth. A relevant goal means having significant and demonstrable bearing on the matter at hand. A goal to run a marathon in the next six months has no bearing on your goal of setting up a spiritual practice to help you connect with your Higher Self and disciplining yourself to your spiritual life this month. This goal must be worthwhile and you must decide if it is right for you at this point in your process.

TIME BOUND – time bound means setting a time frame to complete your goal. For me this can be a little sticky. While I know you must set a time frame to complete your goal; for example, tomorrow, next week, next month or even next year, you must be more specific than that. Give it a solid date, and if you have to adjust that date, don't beat yourself up. By giving yourself a solid day you will have a sense of urgency and a good target to shoot toward.

SOME COMMON MISTAKES OF GOAL SETTING ARE:

- ✔ Making the goal too big. This can cause you to lose interest or feel overwhelmed. If you have a large goal, break it down into small increments. After all, you can eat an elephant if you eat it one bite at a time.

- ✔ Setting too many. This can cause you to be scattered and lose focus. You will be overwhelmed and will end up not reaching any of your goals.

- ✔ Not specific enough. If you are not specific enough it will be difficult to accomplish your goal because you won't have a clear road map.

- ✔ Being too rigid. When setting dates and deadlines, you must realize that things can shift and change which may affect your timeframe, so you must be willing to be flexible and make the necessary adjustments. A setback doesn't mean failure. You must be willing to make the necessary changes to your goal and get back in the saddle.

✔ The biggest mistake one can make is not writing it down. If you don't write down your goal it's just in your head along with all of the other 70,000 thoughts that pass through each day. Writing it down helps you to see it clearly and to really get committed. Also, tell someone about your goal, some one you trust and who will support you in achieving your goals.

THIS IS NOT FOR THE FAINT OF HEART

Getting your time frame together takes work, and lots of it. Your coach can and should be there to support you through every step of this process. While flushing out the issue and the project you want to include in your coaching experience, you can and will uncover some pretty deep issues that have been buried for years. That is why the process of establishing your timeline is not for the faint of heart. You will be calling upon some of your deepest emotions as you sort out the parts of your life that need fixing.

You will be learning to manage your time better, which may be a foreign concept to you. You can feel overwhelmed, and at times confused and scared. Learn to break up more time-consuming tasks with shorter, easier tasks. Give yourself permission to think of the shorter task as mini rewards instead of work. Do something nice for yourself—actually reward yourself once you have completed a group of small tasks toward completing the bigger goal. You are not only learning to manage time but you are learning to manage yourself. This is a tall order, especially if you have been living from an unconscious level as most people do. Almost ninety-eight percent of people live unconsciously. They live their lives on automatic. Most have forgotten or never knew who they truly are, so they don't really know how they are calling forth their experiences and what they are creating. They don't realize that we are all Divine expressions of God and that we are co-creators with the Universe. When you understand who you truly are, managing yourself will become a much easier task.

THE END GAME

What is your end game? What is this timeline all about? You have set your agenda, you know where you want to go, you've put together your most important goals, so now you come to the end game and have some real forward motion. What is going to be different and what is going to change in your life? These are legitimate questions that will lead you to understand and shape what the end game looks like. If you truly want something different to happen in your life and you want to be changed at the end of this process then you must change the behavior or the end game will stay the same.

When one continues to do the same thing over and over and expects the outcome to somehow be miraculously different, well, I've heard that you call that *insanity*. You can't change a negative situation in your life by just saying you want it to change. The situation won't change by wishing it away either. You have to do something totally different, something that is from the extreme opposite direction, and something you have never done before. For most people that's hard. It's really difficult to go beyond their comfort zone to change the situation or make the life shift.

What you must realize is that permanent change can be challenging. The mindset that got you into the negative situation will not be the mindset that gets you out. The mind that is in control is unacceptable and will not facilitate a change of behavior. I call that mind the monkey mind, because it is constantly chattering, filling your head with useless data and keeping your mind cluttered. It is possible that you may come up with some temporary solutions, solutions that give you momentary satisfaction, but for real change, lasting change, the monkey mind will not get you there. In those moments that things seem resolved you'll experience some peace, some joy and maybe even some elation that creates a sense of moving forward. These feelings will last for a week, or even a few months and WHAM it hits you and you're right back where you started. NO forward movement, NO progress, NO joy, NO peace, and your situation is worse than ever.

If you truly want something drastically different in your life, then you must do something drastically different.

The behavior and the thinking that got you into the negative situation will not get you out of it. Think about it; your best thinking got you into the situation and it is that very thinking that is keeping you there. It is almost like you have to distrust yourself and your own judgment—and you do, especially the behavior and thoughts coming from the monkey mind chatter—that you must ignore. Do the opposite of what you normally do even if it scares you. Be still, go within and trust your inner guidance to lead you out of the darkness. It takes drastic measures to have real change and to move you forward. What the end game looks like is up to you, and your coach is there to help you create your reality to look just the way you desire.

TIME

Time; what is this element that occupies
my mind that I am so caught up with?
Time; is it real or is it an illusion, a figment of
my mind and imagination?
We spend our lives trying to manipulate time for
any vocation, without motivation
Time is misunderstood, it is misused and
often by so many, time is abused
In the spiritual realm there is no time,
it is only in my thoughts, only in my mind

Time is only in this realm, it is only in this dimension
Time weighs you down; it slows your vibrations
so much I won't mention
Time lulls your brain and dulls your senses
causing tremendous mental tension
Time dulls the shine of your mind causing your life to be
null, your thoughts to be blind
In the spiritual realm there is no time,
it is only a pearl I hold in the center of my world

Time doesn't wait for you to get it right,
it keeps moving on from day to night
Time is a placeholder; it's a stopgap measure
for something bigger, something bolder
We can spend it, we can use it, but once it's gone
we can't change it or re-choose it.

It can be spent silently, it can be spent unaware, yet
rarely do we have much to spare
In the spiritual realm there is no time, it's simply
a learning device for the miracle mind

Time ushers in the life of a new baby; it erases
all evidence of birth trauma and rage
Time etches in the lines and wrinkles of old age,
it holds the secrets of the ancient sage
Time is a linear life, a straight line to collect
memories and treasures of pain and pleasure
Time slips in and life slips out in a twinkling of an eye,
carrying our soul over rivers of doubt
In the spiritual realm there is no time, it's an illusion,
a slight of hand bringing on the conclusion

It flows like water from eon to eon
moving uninterrupted and uncorrupted
It holds memories of loves and of losses, time spans,
roads and bridges that one crosses
Time is used for the greater good of so many
and at other times for the worst of so few
Time etches and molds the illusions that we hold in our
hearts and minds becoming confusion
In the spiritual realm there is no time,
there is no rhythm there is no rhyme

Time outruns the rivers, it ebbs and flow with the oceans
and sweeps over the mountains

Time feeds and nourishes every plant and flows freely
through forests like a Grecian fountain
Time is at the beginning of galaxies and will be
the end of falsehoods and fallacies
Time is oil for the Belt of Orion, it transverses the Pleiades
and is the pulse of the Universe
Yet, in the spiritual realm there is no time,
it's just a dream, a focused light beam holding us in
separation from the Oneness/The God/Goddess/
The All That Is.
For great Time log examples go to....

3

HOW YOU GOT WHERE YOU ARE TODAY

hings are never what they seem. There are multiple layers of unfelt emotions that are never felt but protect the core of our beings. The vast majority of people are not even aware that they have spent their entire lives teaching themselves how to disconnect from their feelings. In fact, this describes the standard rule of thumb for most of mankind. Our species learns this as a babe. We are told not to cry after a certain age. Little boys are told to suck it up, that boys don't cry. When we are upset, we are taught that it's not polite to show anger, especially in public. We're told it's not ladylike to express anger, and we suppress it, remaining subdued. When something makes us happy, we are supposed to feel joy but we are so afraid to be too happy because we fear the happiness won't last too long. We don't really allow ourselves to truly feel the joy and happiness of the event. When we lose a loved one, we're taught that grieving is healthy but we're told not to grieve too long. Because we don't see death as a part of life, many of our feelings are held within after the loss.

SOME HISTORY

Some clients have told me they were never hugged or kissed by either parent so they don't know what emotion they should feel. Yet this doesn't mean they don't have emotions within them. This simply means they are taught how to suppress these emotions and not feel them. It is mind-blowing to me that so many people don't realize they're completely out-of-touch with their emotions. Certain cultures are notorious for being completely disconnected. After all, in these cultures, logic is deeply rooted. These people are predestined to live their entire lives depersonalizing and disassociating from anyone and anything that gets too close to them. They hold no desire to have influential emotions and no need to correct this behavior. These cultures have little desire to change; they aren't exactly equipped to enact such a change. However, it's important to note that the younger generations are beginning to try.

In some cultures showing emotions is strictly forbidden and frowned upon, and sometimes seen as a sign of weakness. Our children learn that showing any sign of sentiment or sensation publicly, and even in their homes at times, are prohibited. Some of us grew up without ever hearing the words "I love you"; it just wasn't said to each other in the family.

The vast majority of my clients simply skim the top layer of their emotions. They bring in only a small amount of emotions and react to the least amount of sensation. They are completely detached from the deeper levels of their feelings and emotions. Because of this detachment, the client doesn't know how he ended up where he is: in trouble in his life. This doesn't mean, of course, that he is indifferent to his life or that he has a lack of interest in others or others' feelings. To the contrary, people who are indifferent don't care about anyone or anything and can be passive or passive aggressive, and this is not true for most of the people we encounter.

EMOTIONAL DETACHMENT

Many people live their entire lives completely detached from everyone and everything because they have experienced some form of childhood trauma, abuse or emotional abandonment. Take, for instance, a little girl who experienced emotional abuse daily. She displays fear and keeps her distance from everyone. If we look at the child's struggle at the deepest level, I believe the central component lies in the gap between her parents' or caregivers' declaration of love towards her and the child's secret; usually an unspoken belief that her parents don't love her because they abuse her. The child resolves this problem the only way she can. She refuses to allow herself to feel anything and at this point she also refuses to participate in what she perceives as the harmful cycle of emotional abuse. Because of this, the child stops feeling any of her emotions deeply. This leads to a form of detachment. The child will grow into a woman who experiences everything from a distance. Her unrealistic self-image will be like that of a sensible philosopher who has little need for "insignificant emotions". She will possess stealth-like admiration for others who have the ability to feel and control their emotions, yet openly she will hold them in contempt, unable to contain her disdain and envy. Her life will reflect the high values she places on her freedom and independence. She will use all arguments to prove their necessity in anyone's life. When the emotional thermostat begins to rise in romantic or friendly relationships, she will distance herself, leaving her partner with great frustration and confusion. This cycle will repeat itself over and over again in her life.

An infinite number of women like her often get married or enjoy long-term relationships. Unfortunately an emotional abyss always exists between them and their partners. It's important to note that she can feel some emotions in certain situations. However, she feels them under very guarded and controlled conditions. She fears these emotions and prefers to keep them private. She's built layer upon layer of walls to protect her emotions, as if her emotions are precious jewels. As long as her emotions are locked away this woman will never really experience what it feels like to connect with another person, or to share her emotions with another person.

Many of us have experienced some form of disconnect. However we're not usually aware of this detachment from our emotions. *If one is to really become attached in life again, connecting and understanding our feelings and emotions is paramount.* If one cannot decipher their feelings they are out of touch with their inner Spirit. After all, it is through that connection that our Higher Self communicates with us -- through our feelings. So one must begin their personal journey and embark on the exploration of their values, beliefs and behavior, and then they will find themselves understanding how they resulted in detachment very quickly. You'll understand that getting to the core of your disconnect is necessary in order to be emotionally whole again.

THE GOD FACTOR

There are three ways in which God speaks to us. The first is through our feelings. We get these unshakeable feelings about a person, place or thing – that is God speaking. The second is through our thoughts. Suddenly a thought will pop into your head from nowhere; it's not always logical and most times it doesn't make sense –that is God speaking. The third is the physical word and/or world. You see a sign, or a friend says something that sparks a fire within you, or you read something in a book or see a movie that give you a message. Feeling is the purest and most uncontaminated form of communication that one can receive from God. It is the mainline, and the first line of communication. You can trust it with every fiber of your being.

Have you ever had a hunch, a gut feeling, or just an overwhelming feeling to do something? That feeling is the Universe speaking to you. You must listen. "Follow Your First Mind" is one of my Estherisms. If by chance you are not connected to your emotions and feelings and haven't learned to trust your feelings you will miss the messages God is sending you through that source. The next form of communication will show up in a thought. Thought is not as reliable as feeling because it can become contaminated with other thoughts very easily and one may second-guess the message. Unless you have trained yourself to follow your first mind, or the first thought that comes to you no matter how unrealistic it may seem, you will not recognize that the Universe is talking to you. The third way of receiving the message from the Universe is through the word or the world. This occurs when someone verbally gives you the message. Alternatively, you read it in a book, see it on television or experience it through an event.

The following story shows a very emotional and traumatic time in my life during which I found myself exposed to all three forms of the Universe's communication.

GOD IS TALKING

When I got the call that my sister was in the hospital and had coded twice, I knew I had to be on the next thing smoking— the next car, the next airplane, whatever. My mind was so discombobulated I couldn't even book my ticket. My inner voice said, "Be Still". I went to my altar and sat there trying to be still, but my mind was moving at the speed of light and I couldn't still it. I got up again and started trying to pack, but my inner spirit was saying, "Be Still". I called a friend in Texas who worked for the airlines and woke her up to ask her to help me get a ticket. She told me to give her an hour and she would call me back. My mind was swirling and twirling with all kinds of thoughts and fears. Would I get there in time? Could I go on if she didn't make it,? How much time did I really have to get there? The voice within me spoke to me again, "Be Still". I went back to my seat in front of my altar and sat there. I began to pray and breathe deeply. As my breathing slowed and each breath began to be drawn out I could feel a blanket of calmness enfold me. The Spirit within me spoke again and said, "Her sickness is not unto death". The Spirit again spoke to me and said, "Put in a return date". I got up and went back to my computer, put the return date into my search for a ticket, and a multitude of tickets popped up. By the time my friend called back, I had already booked my ticket and was on the next plane leaving.

My flight went very smoothly. I spent most of the time praying and sleeping. Once I got to California, I went straight to the hospital to see my sister. She was barely breathing. She was strapped to oxygen and her face was completely gray. She looked very, very weak. I leaned over her and said, "We are going to create something different." I don't know why I said that to her. She looked up at me through tear-filled eyes and shook her head in agreement. The next morning I got her out of bed so she could sit in her chair to eat breakfast. This didn't happen without her protest, of course. But she did it. In my mind and heart, I knew she would be all right. The Universe had spoken to me before I left home. I also knew I was going to help my sister regain her strength and mobility. She couldn't even stand or walk on her own anymore. Here was my sister whom I loved more than life itself, unable to fully function. Yet in all of this, I knew this was not about my sister. It was about me. My sister's illness was just a vehicle for some new awareness to unfold for me. Wow, I had no idea about what was to come.

Generally, when I go to California to visit my sister, I am faced with many old emotions and family issues. At the time of her hospitalization, at least twelve other family members were living in her house. I knew that each one of my family members would play a different role in my sister's recovery—or lack of recovery. They depended on her to take care of everything house-related, even though she was physically and mentally unable to do little more than keep herself alive. At that time, not one of the twelve stepped up to take on my sister's task of running the house. I automatically assumed the role of her champion, taking on all of the problems and issues of discontent in my sister's house. Over the years of being her champion, it took its toll on me. This time it was different. I knew I had to make some different choices. My spiritual and physical health depended on it.

Once I got her discharged and settled at home the issues were not just confined within that house. Rather they extended to everything concerning her. My sister's medical care was not the best, but I chose to get the best out of the worst. I became her medical advocate, pledging to make her more than just a number in the system. We were able to move mountains with help and direction from the Universe. I was able to get her an appointment to see a doctor so she could get the medication and the medical equipment she needed urgently so she would be able to sleep safely. It took a constant and consistent effort to get things done for her but I stayed in Spirit and stayed focused until it was done. During this time of daily working with doctors, medical staff and coordinators, the issues with other family members continued to mount.

During this same time my youngest sister decided she would go to the hospital and have surgery, which meant she could not help with the recovery of my older sister. I turned to my spiritual community at the school I was attending to pray with me and send me light and energy. My school community came through and their prayers were felt as I nursed and tended to my sister as well as to her household.

I was being shown so many different things all at once and my soul was being opened up to new understandings about who I was and what my immediate family-driven purpose was. I learned to listen and to get still so I could see the unseen and hear the unspoken. I could understand what I was feeling and immerse myself deep into my emotions for the messages. I was able to talk to my older sister in a way I never had before. I was able to let her know that her life was in her own hands and she had to take full responsibility for what was happening in her life. She had to choose life if she wanted to stay here on Earth. It was one of the hardest conversations I ever had to have but I was able to stand in the truth of the conversation. I said what I needed to say in love and from my heart center and she understood. She showed me she understood by doing things for herself immediately.

When I returned home I had to attend school on that weekend. I had just spent a month in California nursing my sister back to health. On that Friday night, I went to the microphone to thank my community for their prayer and support while I was away and to share the emotional and spiritual experiences I had with my family. I was so clear and focused; I could feel my oneness with the Universe all over me as I shared the insights and new understandings I found in California. When I got home, I was still energized and feeling this heightened sense of connection to the

Universe and I couldn't get to sleep. As I tried to relax and get to sleep, I couldn't even get to REM sleep. It seemed like every hour on the hour I was awake looking at the clock with all these thoughts swirling in my head. It was about 3:30 a.m. and I decided to get up and write down the thoughts that were floating around in my head. The poem below, "You Are", is a result of those thoughts.

The next morning our class went to a church service to support one of our faculty members who delivered the message. This particular church was very spirited. The service started off with Praise and Worship Service. The Praise and Worship Service was led by a set of identical female twins. The service was moving along and the Spirit flowed freely throughout the congregation. One of the twins began to cry out, "You Are". She just kept saying it over and over, as if she couldn't help herself. As she repeated the phrase with such strong emotions, I knew the message the night before came directly from the Universe/God.

YOU ARE

You are my first light dawning, my bright and morning star
You are the stream of love that fills
all space everywhere near and far
You are the sunshine and the rain;
you are in the depth of a mother's pain
You are that place of possibilities at the center
and core of my improbabilities
Your are the peace that I find at the center of a star—
the stillness of my chaotic mind
You are all --That is you are my everything,
the grand architect—the great alchemist

You are the lover of my soul, the sweet elixir of love;
you are a mind regulator and a heart fixer
You are the vibrations that stir my senses,
awaken my soul as the early dawn breaks
You are the essence that makes the very earth
shake, tremble and quake
You are the smooth and gentle ripples that a rock makes
when dropped in a placid lake
You are the roaring power of the waves
that breaks with the tide as it ebbs and flows
You are my courageousness, you are my fortress,
and you are my consciousness

You are the essence of each breath I breathe
like the wind blowing quietly through the trees

You are my knowledge, you are my truth
and you are my wisdom—unfolding, beholding
You are the great thoughts that transcend my mind
growing stronger with time
You are the fibers of truth woven in my being,
giving me sparks of sublime divinity
You are the filter that sifts the chaos from my brain,
making all things clear and very plain
You are in my laughter, my joy, and my pain;
you are in my tears and the conqueror of my fears.

You are Abba, my Father, Jehovah, my Lord,
Jehovah-Nissi, my banner,
You are Jehovah-Jireh, my Provider Jehovah-Rophe,
my Healer, El Elyon, the Most High
You are Elohim, the Creator, El Shaddai,
God All Mighty, Yahweh, My Savior
Yes—You are God Alone.

RECONCILIATION WITH SELF

I learned long ago that the first step to healing is acknowledgement. Once you have embarked upon the path of understanding how you got where you are, that's when the work truly begins. When you can acknowledge that the hurt has occurred and that the abuse happened through you and not to you then you can begin the process of forgiveness. Forgiveness is something that is entirely left to you. The coach can support and help you understand that but ultimately it is your decision. As your forgiveness process proceeds, you find yourself in a position to reconcile with that part of yourself that has been wounded and/or abused. In the general sense, reconciliation is usually two people coming together in mutual respect and understanding. But the reconciliation I speak of here requires only your acceptance. You are the only one that can bring both parts of yourself, your Higher-Self and wounded child, together for forgiveness to facilitate the healing process. Although reconciliation may follow forgiveness, it is possible for you to forgive yourself without reconciling the two splintered parts of yourself.

Reconciliation with yourself provides the path to healing the hurt that can't be healed through forgiveness. Forgiveness is a powerful tool and it is a choice you can make when it's right for you.

Forgiveness is a powerful tool; it is a choice you can make that can lead you to greater well-being. Ultimately, it will lead you to the reconciliation with yourself and better relationships with others throughout your life. A paradigm shift occurs when you reconcile with yourself and you begin to see your world through different lenses. You begin to accept yourself fully and wholly with all of your flaws. You will no longer treat yourself with harshness and humiliation. You no longer hold yourself in contempt. You do not judge or hold others in contempt either. You will find yourself loving yourself and loving others naturally.

No longer will you feel self-hatred because you will have managed to transcend yourself to live in harmony with the entire universe.

WHAT HAPPENS WHEN THERE IS NO RECONCILIATION?

When people find no reconciliation with "self," they can and usually will wear their hurt like a badge of honor. They become the hurt, even if they have gone through a forgiveness process. The hurt infiltrates every aspect of their lives; every decision, every thought. All of their encounters and relationships are about the hurt. Some people even make this hurt a way of life. The hurt becomes their identity and they don't know who they are without it.

TOOL FOR FORGIVENESS:

FORGIVE

FIRST acknowledge what has happened in your life that warrants forgiving. Alternately, acknowledge the person or the situation that requires forgiveness.

OWN your actions by taking responsibility for any part that you played to bring about the situation or anything you did to contribute to the issue. Accept the responsibility for where you find yourself.

REVIEW your situation; think about what decisions were made that got you to this point and why you made them. Think about the actions and choices you made that brought about the situation. At this point, you have to be completely honest with yourself, even if it hurts. You may find that you are almost too ashamed to admit or own up to the part you played in the situation. But own it you must. This is the turning point of the process; this is the point of release and relief.

GROW from this new knowledge about yourself, and give yourself a break. Don't be too hard or judgmental of yourself. We all make mistakes. Don't stay in the valley too long; be kind to yourself and understand you are not alone in this process. God/The Universe is always there to support you and comfort you during this time of self-examination.

INVEST in yourself with time through meditation or contemplation. Infuse yourself and the situation with some positive energy. Allow yourself to rise to a higher vibration by letting go of the old negative thoughts.

VALUE the opportunity to correct the situation or issue. This is a blessing in disguise. You may not be able to see it, but you have the opportunity to turn things around in your life. You have the chance to bring enlightenment to others involved in the situation or to be the catalyst for change.

ENJOY the situation and the process of forgiving yourself and others. Use this as an opportunity to understand your relationship with God/The Universe. Enjoy the freedom it brings of being unencumbered by any negative emotions. You are free to redesign your life.

4

GOING DEEPER AND MOVING FORWARD

When a client makes the decision to enlist a life coach, they are looking for results. At this point of the process the client is ready to dig deep, and to go within to find the hidden issues and information. They want to see some results on their path, and they believe they are willing to do anything.

Generally, I see clients that are willing and ready to deal with the surface issues. Unfortunately, they aren't ready to deal with the deeper issues. Sometimes it takes months of sessions before we make a breakthrough and get some forward motion. Note that at this stage the partnership between coach and client must be solid, strong and sturdy for the long haul.

Many of the stories that will come forth during this time have been buried deep within the recesses of your mind for numerous years. The work to be done is crucial to your healing; however, the process is one of the hardest things you will ever deal with in your life, but it will change your life forever. No matter the issue, from child abuse to infidelity, rape to self-mutilation, even a major illness. It really doesn't matter what category the issue falls into, the first step toward your healing is self-acknowledgment. All of the pain, shame, guilt and blame can be resolved and released through this process.

This process is critical because it holds many land mines. You can and do get stuck here. It is the job of the coach to support you as you dig deeper into your past and uncover these memories of shame, pain and guilt. The coach is there to hold the space, and create a safe harbor to explore and extract whatever knowledge or lessons are found there.

Being in the deep valley of one's mind can be a scary place. Many get lost or stuck here; they can take on a whole new persona based on the abuse that occurred. They arrange their whole lives around the issue; they put it on like a suit or carry it like a ball and chain around their ankle. Sometimes they pile on the pounds to hide behind, thinking no one can see them now, or they starve themselves through anorexia because they can't truly see themselves. They bring this abuse persona to every new adventure and lead off every new introduction with it as well. They cannot separate who they are from the fabricated abuse persona. Getting stuck in the valley is not an option, therefore, you must be willing to identify your own path that will lead you up and out of the valley and, ultimately, forward.

A PERSONAL EXPERIENCE OF ABUSE

Now, I will share a story here about my own abuse persona, what it looked like to me and how I overcame it.

I had just taken on a new job; it was a promotion for me but there was a caveat that came with the promotion. At this job, I was given the opportunity to take public properties and turn them into profitable sites. This was something that had never been done before. I developed the idea and presented it to my department director. He liked it and gave me his blessing. The next hurdle was to convince all of the other departments involved that this would work. Therefore, I had to put in many hours selling it to other department heads before I got the green light. Needless to say, the pressure was on. All eyes were on me. I had to produce; I had to make these properties profitable. I worked late on weekends. I ate, slept, and walked this project. I was consumed and obsessed because I had something to prove. I never felt worthy or that I belonged in the ranks of the successful. I always felt that I just wasn't good enough and I had to constantly prove myself. I just wanted to be liked, but I didn't like myself. I knew that a lot of people expected me to fail and that only fueled my insecurities. I allowed these beliefs to be my abuser and I pushed and worked myself into a major illness.

ACKNOWLEGEMNT: THE FIRST STEP

It was the first week of November in 1994; I lay motionless in a hospital bed with tubes connected to every opening of my body. This included an oxygen tank to help me breathe. I could feel the sunlight streaming in through the fingerprint-smudged glass in the windowpane. I could only imagine what activities took place beyond the frame: cars traveling here and there carrying healthy people wherever they wanted to go; delivery people keeping the hospital supplied with equipment and products. I was in this position because of my inability to recognize my self-inflected pain. I had allowed myself to suffer in constant pain for a whole month until I could barely breathe. It was only then that I finally acknowledged something was seriously wrong. I had been in the hospital for eight days, fighting for every breath.

The doctor's face was grim as he clinically uttered my prognosis. Something like, "You've lost a quarter of your right lung due to the blood clot sitting there so long," were the words I remember from my purple haze. Then an unexpected smile graced his face. This smile was a rare, yet inspiring phenomenon. He interjected, "But, with proper exercise, you will regain your health and be able to breathe normally again." In my mind, the phrase "proper exercise" equated to good health and the ability to breathe normally again. That was the turning point for me.

MY JOURNEY BEGINS

Fresh out of the hospital, my recovery began at a snail's pace. I couldn't climb a flight of stairs without gasping to catch my breath. Fatigued was a constant state of being that I refused to become accustomed to. Funny enough, my recovery period was nowhere near the estimated time of arrival back into the land of health. I just kept remembering what the doctor had told me, with exercise, I could become whole again, I was constantly replaying his message in my mind. The belief that this body of mine could rejuvenate itself with a lot of effort kept me on the road to my destination.

I joined a gym with the goal to exercise for thirty minutes three times a week. This prescription seems to be the latest pop fitness guru's answer to a healthy lifestyle. I had not taken into account the gross number of pounds that made their way onto my body during my illness, nor did I consider the effects these pounds would have on my ability to exercise. I was undaunted by the challenge. Instead, I purchased every fitness magazine on the supermarket shelves. Footlocker For Women was a foreign land, but I waded through and exited with a wealth of knowledge and excess debt on overextended credit cards. After taking inventory of the total situation, I found myself overwhelmed. There seemed to be no easy exit from this oversized unfamiliar body.

Panic became my intimate companion. It greeted me as I rose from the sheets, constantly hovering like a bird of prey. Any little setback launched a waterfall of tears instead of an avalanche of encouragement, which I needed. I was fat, out of breath, and depressed by the reality of my life. Alone in this pursuit, I knew that if it was to be it was up to me but I didn't have the strength or the know-how I desperately needed to proceed. How would I ever reverse this situation? Dieting alone wasn't the remedy. It only left me hollow and cranky—not the best characteristics to win friends and influence others to help me. Exercise had to be the key. This was the message my inner voice kept running on a loop inside my head. I was compelled to listen.

THE GYM

My first trip to the gym was like stepping onto the stage for my first performance in the school play. It was intimidating and strangely invigorating. My heart fluttered and skipped beats. My old friend, panic, held vigil without fail; I hadn't gotten rid of him yet. Most of the women present had bodies like model athletes. They were jumping around in the aerobic classes with barely any leotards on. The men as well as the women had their gluteus that was indeed maximus, round and tight on full display. I was mesmerized by the possibilities before me. After all, the women I most often associated with were in relatively poor health and far too comfortable within their married lives to pay serious attention to their bodies. Role models they were not.

The men in the gym appeared to be products of an artist's imagination. Even the buxom babes, and there were many, gave causes for an extended stare. Suddenly, I felt like an outsider, an intruder during a ritual at the temple of the Sacred Order of the Perfect Body. Passing through the labyrinth, trying my best to avoid my reflection in the multitude of mirrors, I felt the warm liquid substance hurdle my lower lids and expose itself in a stream-like fashion down my cheeks, around my nostrils, through the microscopic hairs that lined my upper lip and take flight off my chin. I was crying. I wanted to run away, but where would I go? I couldn't hide from myself. I was too embarrassed to make eye contact with the worshipers, afraid they would see me as a blasphemer. I was ignorant to their ways. I sat in the locker room for what seemed an eternity, nearly falling asleep. After crying myself into exhaustion, I took a deep breath, exhaled and sat silently. I recalled my mantra, "Proper exercise equates to good health."

With the power of the Universe compelling me, I stepped into the arena and laid eyes on my new best friend; the treadmill. The treadmill would lead me down the path of righteousness. Initially, sixty seconds was my threshold before I had to stop, catch my breath, and rest. I would not, however, be denied. Therefore, I persisted until I worked my way up to ten consecutive minutes on my very first day! The next day I returned and was able to conquer up to twelve minutes. The next day I did fifteen. I was on my way and I was proud of myself. This new relationship with the treadmill was difficult and frustrating, I felt awkward and backward. I remained determined to work my way up to thirty minutes. Thankfully, that day came quickly Although I could walk for thirty minutes consecutively, I still experienced great difficulty breathing. My breath didn't come easily, but my determination was inflated and subtly edged out my old companion—panic. As I continued to play my mantra in my head, my heart was lifted and my soul was inspired, or rather, in-spirit. I knew I was on the path to wholeness.

"One day at a time," was my cliché motto. I knew I could swallow the ocean one sip at a time. The gym became my place of solace. It held and comforted me in a way that my soul needed at that time. The physical results were slow and hidden, although my broken spirit benefitted immensely from this ritual of discipline. The first year of this new relationship with exercise left a lot to be desired, at least in my appearance. Some days I was slow as molasses, which was okay. I just had to keep moving.

MOVING TO THE NEXT LEVEL

To promote significant results, I changed gyms and enlisted the expertise of a personal trainer on a bi-weekly basis; my progress remained slow. It seemed my body wasn't finished suffering from my previous illness. My body was holding on to every ounce of fat. I had to undergo two additional surgeries in as many years before my body gave in, and through it all I continued to worship at the gym temple. When I couldn't get there, I worshiped in nature along the wooded paths, or just on the city streets. I remained encouraged because I had now been initiated into the higher order of gym junkies.

After the final surgery in August 1996, I attended the fall season all-natural body building competition. This was an opportunity for me to support fellow worshipers from my gym since we had several entries. Our gym had an excellent reputation for entering top-notch talent. At this show I saw women my age and older on stage in phenomenal shape. It was an epiphany. They looked healthy and vivacious; they didn't look anything like I imagined—definitely not like the images of 1980s steroid-laced bodybuilders. I can do this, I thought to myself. This was my vehicle to success. Little did I know what the women on that stage had been through to get there; I had no idea what they had to endure. I didn't know what degree of commitment it took or to what extent they had sacrificed for that one moment in time. I was oblivious to the grueling hours of sweat and pain required to whip their mortal bodies into those heavenly silhouettes that stood before us that night. Because of my excitement, enthusiasm, and desire I would soon learn their secrets.

I spoke with the gym's resident bodybuilding trainer about preparing me for a show by April of 1997. My starting weight was a whopping 265 pounds. My trainer had a very straightforward style and spared none of my feelings when explaining what it would take to get me completion ready. There were four other women interested too, but the other women had competed in a few shows before. They were already on the path and knew the regime. My trainer was also a world-class bodybuilder and power lifter. She told me that power lifting strengthens and builds muscle, and I would have to power lift if I wanted to get faster results. She explained the appropriate bodybuilding diet and the detailed individual exercise regiments. It was up to us to adhere to our diet and persevere through our exercise regimen.

Our next group meeting was in February. This was an evaluation of our progress. My weight had not dropped as fast as I had hoped; I still had forty excess pounds. This was a disappointment to both the trainer and me. I knew I would not get to my goal weight by April. The trainer knew too, but still encouraged me to keep working. The trainer went on to work closely with the other women because they had realistic possibilities of qualifying for the show in April. During the two months until the April show was over I was left on my own to continue on the road to success. I faced difficulty and much self-doubt along the way. My mind played awful tricks on me. It wasn't good enough to be diligent some of the time. I had to stick to the program and the diet every day. Some days I just didn't think I could do another work out, but I always did. I didn't think I could eat another chicken breast, hard-boiled egg white, or power bar, but I always complied. Frequently, I partnered up with whoever would work out with me—just for the support. Any support would do, it helped me keep my enthusiasm up. Most times, however, I had to do it alone. Steel barbells and me, lifting, pulling and pushing. The act was a part of the tribal loyalty. Increased difficulty only strengthened my resolve to master the bench press, cable cross, and squat platform. My mind was steeped in the physical fitness culture. I experienced euphoria, a seemingly ordained re-birth. The results I envisioned and prayed for became reality. The more results materialized, the harder I worked. One of my teammates qualified and won first place in her weight class at the April show.

GOING DEEP AND MOVING FORWARD

In May, the trainer turned her attention back to me. We set a new goal, and she took me through a new workout step by step—ascending thousands of steps, walking hundreds of miles. I logged unimaginable hours of sit-ups, push-ups and lunges never forgetting that every deep and deliberate inhale was a gift from God. I was experiencing human evolution —although mostly I just felt like I was going to die from all of the aches and pains as my body went through this transformation.

My trainer was so impressed with my determination that she committed her full array of training skills to my new goal. The desire that arose from deep within me was my Passion. It stimulated my soul. Now the real work was to begin. I could see the goal looming before me. I was up at the crack of dawn for two hours of cardiovascular exercise in the morning and another two hours of a full free weight workout for the evening. My only luxury was the sweet smell of bubbles swirling around me in my bath each evening. This was about the time I researched Body Shop stock prices. The sales clerk at my nearest location knew me by name. Epsom salt was another friendly pain reliever. I discovered muscle groups that I had no knowledge of possessing nor could I pronounce them. It was during this time of reformation that I educated myself more deeply about this mysterious house of the spirit. I knew I was on a spiritual journey; I was communing with God, the Universe, every time I stepped into that gym.

People began to take notice. My body changes were undeniable. I received comments from family members and friends alike. People questioned me about my health. Why was I losing so much weight? Was I sick? Was I obsessed? Did I have an eating disorder? What program was I on? They would say things like, "Don't lose any more weight. You're getting too small. You look sick. Your losing your butt, and we are going to take away your 'sister card' because you have no butt left." It was a strange feeling to have people I knew making such negative statements to me. I thought my friends and associates would be more supportive, happy for me and proud of me. Instead they made me feel like I was doing something wrong or damaging to my body. People I had known for many years were passing me on the street without as much as a hello. I would speak, and then with shock in their eyes, they would respond, "Esther I didn't know that was you." It was as if I had suddenly become someone else. There were times I felt invisible because at events and networking meetings I could move among people I knew and not be noticed. Even when I took the time to explain what I was doing and how much it meant to me people still tried to make me feel as if I had done something wrong. It didn't dissuade me though, it only made me more determined to reach my goal.

I felt like a new person—an improved version. I was running twenty-five miles a week—something I once thought impossible. I felt like I had taken fifteen years off my age. I was hooked. I was committed. I was dedicated and I was healthy and whole. Exercise was the answer but not just for my health, but for the discipline I needed to connect to my Higher Self.

MY MOMENT IN TIME

My goal date was fast approaching. I was on target but not completely satisfied with how things were shaping up. As the date drew closer, I became more dissatisfied with how I looked. By then, however, I didn't really know what to look at any longer. My ability to gauge how I should look in relation to how I did look was distorted. In those moments I understood how women suffer through anorexia without seeing the problem. Reality is a relative phenomenon. As I pressed on, my trainer was there every step of the way, encouraging me, supporting me, and pushing me to the last repetition in my last set.

Suddenly the tortured discourse and extended regiments ceased. The night that dreams were made of had arrived. It was show time. October 24, 1997, one full year from the bodybuilding show that ignited the fire within me. Ninety-one pounds lighter, countless hours in the gym and finally there, I prepared to mount that very same stage. The very same stage where that dream had been born in me, where my eyes first fixed on my destiny. My heart pounded and skipped beats at the same time. My skin was aglow from the endless stream of nervous sweat. I took it all in, watching my competition prepare for the battle. A lot of stretching and pumping took place in the wings. I was as prepared as I could be. Stage make-up was on, bronzing solution had been carefully applied hours earlier, and my hand-sewn bikini costume was tucked and tapped in all the right places.

My thoughts continued to race; "Have I done everything I can do to prepare for this?" I wondered. The answer was yes. Panic and self-doubt were not invited to this occasion. There was no room within me for their presence. My Masters Women category was summoned to the stage. This was it. I stepped on stage and executed my compulsory poses with all the concentration I could muster. The hot stage lights glistened like stars in my eyes. I was hooked. Right, left, center and side, I twisted and tensed my body. This was my opportunity to show off the work I claimed as my own. My body temple was sanctified and consecrated, ready to lay claim to this moment of glory before the precious minutes ticked away.

MY PERSONAL RELATIONSHIP WITH SPIRIT

Although the night did not yield a personal trophy, my team performed well. In the end I did win. I won self-respect and a new healthy relationship with my body. At the end of this road, I found my passion. Every sit-up, push-up and mile that I ran brought me to a higher understanding of my relationship with Spirit. It was about half way through that I realized this was not just a physical journey it was a spiritual one. I knew that if I was to have a disciplined mind to spirit I had to bring my body under submission. The submission I am speaking about here was to be able to say no to food and drink that were not serving my body very well. To say yes to the exercise that had never been a part of my life yet was needed so very badly. I knew this was a spiritual walk. As I took each step, I took it in holy reverence; I knew from whence I'd come and I was blessed. I prayed most of the time when I reached that place of euphoria, prayers of gratitude and thanksgiving.

Time stood still for me; it was as if I'd crossed over into another dimension once I got into my regime. I understood that I had to first conquer my physical body before I could truly connect to my spirit, before I could even hear my Higher Self. So this journey became a kind of ritual, and through this ritual I began to secure a stronger relationship with God.

SOUL WORK - YOU ARE ALWAYS AT CHOICE

The story I shared above was my journey of going deeper and moving forward. I had to be willing to take the plunge with my coach. My coach helped me to dig deeper and move forward. I not only reached my goals but I became acquainted with my Higher Self in a more significant way. Are you willing to take the plunge? Are you willing to go deeper within your innermost dreams, desires and hopes? Do you want your soul to be soothed and made whole? Do you want to accomplish your goals? If the answer is yes then it is at this point of your relationship with the coach that will moves you forward. This is where soul work is done, where you will make choices that will reach the depth of your soul. Only you can determine how far down the rabbit hole you want to go. You are always at choice. You decide how far or how deep you want to explore. Your forward motion will be determined by your willingness to do the work at the soul level. The good news is if you don't like the choice you've made or the direction you're going in while doing this soul-work, you can always make another choice. The bad news is that most people don't realize that they can make another choice. They are so stuck in habitual behavior patterns they can't choose differently. Just know as you embark on this path of healing at the soul level you will be forever changed.

THE SONG OF THE SOUL

In the stillness of the night
when in the city there's not much light.
Lie down, sweet one, and you will hear
a lullaby just beyond your ear.
Listen intently, listen direct,
listen with your soul, without being told.
Hear the melody, every note deep in the heart,
every instrument playing its part.

In the depths of my being
I feel strong vibrations of the soul song.
As I drift and float upon each note
joy abounds and I'm one with sound.
Pulsating and gyrating in the secret,
hidden chambers of my being—my universe.
I feel the melody, I feel each and every note
dancing together never leaving my throat.

In my veins, in my blood stream,
down my spine each note does intertwine.
Strumming my ribs, drumming my tummy
the vibratory sound keeps on humming.
In my vocal cords, behind my eyes
the sensation of this song plays down to my thighs.
Loud and clear nowhere near my ear
I sense every note—still each is so very remote.

Within the gasps of the song of the soul
is held every note of music untold.
My life plays out as melodies from above
floating through me on the wings of a dove.
It matters not from winch you come or
whence you go, the notes play on to and fro.
Beyond human consciousness, beyond human touch
the Song of the Soul is just such.

5

LETTING GO OF THE STORY

*E*veryone sees the world through their own perceptions. I call them filters, and everyone uses filters to perceive the world around them. You have two lenses, one in each eye, that help you focus on information in order for your brain to interpret what the eyes have perceived. The filters are not in the eyes, the filters are in your mind. You create the filter based on the stories you tell yourself while interpreting the information that comes through your eyes. If you have ever worn glasses and they get dirty, you know that the world becomes distorted because you are looking through a film of dirt. Once you clean the dirt off them, your ability to see clearly comes into focus. You could say that the dirt on your glasses is like a filter you have created in your mind and it's not allowing you to see what you are looking at clearly. A story that has no basis in truth is like the dirt on your glasses. So what filters are you living your life through? What is coloring your view of life?

In the above statement I used dirt to describe a filter, but what I'm talking about here is filters in your life that are made up from the stories you tell yourself. A filter can be many things and can be created by many events in your life. Most of the time you are not aware of the filters that are coloring your life; you think the way you're viewing things is normal or correct.

I want to share a story about my daughter.

When she was young we didn't know she couldn't see very well. We were on the hustle and grind of life and it didn't occur to me to have her eyes tested. It wasn't until she was in the fifth grade that her teacher noticed that she couldn't see the chalk board from the back of the classroom and suggested that we have her eyes tested. When she got her new glasses she was so excited that she could see the leaves on the trees and the small details around her like the blades of grass and petals of the flowers in our yard. She was so excited about all of the new and colorful patterns of her clothes and the small things she had never seen before. She said to me that she never knew she couldn't see, she just thought that was how the world was. Her grades began to improve drastically and she became an ardent reader and writer.

That awareness was such a wake-up call for me. I realized at that moment that my child had been going through life not seeing the world clearly and she didn't even know. I felt truly bad; I beat myself

*up mentally and emotionally. I judged myself harshly
and it was a blow to my parenting skills at that time.*

Looking back on that incident, I now know that I did the best I knew how to do at that time in my life. Beating myself up or judging my parenting skills was just a story I was telling myself that had no basis in reality. I felt terrible already and the story about how inept as a parent I was only heaped more coal on the fire. This behavior was my default behavior as a young parent; any mishap or mistake called for self-abuse and self-loathing. I constantly filled my head with stories that had no basis in truth. These stories were born out of my feelings of unworthiness and self-hatred, and not knowing that I had these beliefs, my whole world was being shaped by these stories that I continuously told myself. It didn't matter how many times I told myself to be positive and to think only good thoughts; as long as I was seeing the world through the filters created by the stories I was telling myself, my life could never take an upswing.

Sometimes events happen in our lives that change the way we see the world, and the change may not always be beneficial for us. These events become what I call filters because we form stories in our head about the events. Many of these filters are formed in your early childhood so you are unaware of them, and think that's just how the world appears and how things have always been. You have told yourself the same stories so long that you truly accept them as your truth, and they are just that: your truth.

Every culture has its own traditions and customs. These morals and behaviors help form your filters too. They determine how you see the world. Generally speaking, cultural behaviors are usually fine but when things go wrong through some type of abnormality or abuse, this causes you to form filters for protection and to shield yourself from the pain and hurt of the negative actions. You make up stories that are not as painful as the abuse you're suffering so you can cope and make some sense out of what's happening to you. From these stories you learn how to behave and show up in ways that do not serve you as you grow and go out into the real world. You do things that are self-sabotaging or self-abusive, you allow people to mistreat you and you accept less than you deserve; all because you're seeing the world and yourself through the filters you formed in your early childhood. You are still telling the stories and the stories you created early on in your life are still your truth.

REWRITING THE AGENDA

There are times you may feel that you have no choice, life sucks and you must continue the destructive path you're on. However, at any moment you can make a different choice. That's what rewriting the agenda is all about. That is why I said in the beginning that the agenda is your roadmap and more likely will change once you embark on the journey. I have found that a client's agenda changes along with where they want to go as the coaching session progress. The agenda is a working document, it is fluid, and as you move along your journey you must be open and flexible in the evolving coaching relationship.

Issues will come forth as you work with the coach and you must decide which of these issues are important to you. You must decide which way you want your journey to unfold. When your road map is not accurate, you can get lost and it becomes easy to resort to your default behavior because that behavior is an old friend and you know it so well. Since change is your goal here but it isn't always easy - I would say it isn't easy 99% of the time - slipping back into old behavior can happen to anyone at this point. That's why making the necessary changes to your agenda is so very important at this juncture.

*Estherism: At Any Moment You Can
Make a Different Choice*

What choices are you making or not making? Think about it and consider: at any moment you can make a different choice.

PUT ON YOUR GROWN-UP PANTIES

You might ask, "What does putting panties on have to do with the stories you're telling yourself?" The saying "put on your big girl panties" or your "grown-up panties" is a saying I picked up while in school completing my training to become a Spiritual Life Coach. What it means is life happens, things go wrong, we miscalculate, we don't always get our way, but we have to learn to deal with it, we have to grow up for real and face whatever stories we are telling ourselves. We have to examine the filters we have been seeing the world through. You will need your big girl panties on when you have your Come to Jesus Meeting with yourself. Your big girl panties are your shield, your armor and will help you deal with the knife, shards of glass and any other debris that life throws at you. I had one such experience in 2009 and it wasn't pretty.

COME TO JESUS MEETING

A "Come to Jesus Meeting" is getting called on the carpet, dressed down, or otherwise chewed out in a severe manner; being made to face your demons or the hidden part of yourself that you don't want to face.

I was about to start my second year in my spiritually-based training program and we always started the school year with a week of isolation from our normal lifestyle called summer intensive. This is where we spent concentrated time with our classmates and instructors for the coming year to get ready to do the work. This particular summer intensive had started out pretty normal for me. Things were pretty low key, not too much drama. I always tried to fly below the radar and not get called to the microphone to share. Going to the microphone was an exercise used for us to go and share our experiences about good or bad fortune, our issues, our growth, and/or our lack of growth.

Summer intensive consisted of exercises that brought us face to face with our hidden issues and some that weren't so hidden. I watched each day as different classmates got in touch with their innermost secrets, their triggers and their fears. I chose to sit on the sidelines and operate from my most familiar places of detachment and unavailability. In doing so I would not have to feel any of the negative things that were being sent my way. I was completely unattached from my emotions and I was all right with that; ignorance is bliss and I felt safe and insulated. I had learned to move through life this way and I was doing just fine, so I thought. My filters had always worked for me and I truly believed I was projecting this image of a strong, secure and totally together spiritual woman. But beneath it all a storm was brewing and what I didn't know was that I was wearing the symptoms of that storm on my shelves. All of my insecurities were being projected all over the place, but I stuck to my familiar stories.

I was triggering people all over the place, and since I was so completely detached and unaware, I saw it as their problem. I allowed things to be spoken to me and about me with no real reaction; after all, it wasn't my drama. I didn't understand what these people wanted from me. What in God's name did they expect me to do about someone else's drama? It certainly didn't have anything to do with me, so I thought; again one of the old stories running in my head. When a person is as detached from their emotions as I was it is easy to keep moving through life wreaking havoc in others' lives and not taking responsibility for any of it. My filters were strong and thick; I had become so good at assigning blame to the other person that I didn't even know how to be wrong anymore. I truly believed I was never wrong, at least not when it came to how I treated people.

On the very last day of our summer intensive I sat on the front row, thinking to myself I had gotten through another weeklong session intact. We were at the very end of the day going through the last exercise, and as I sat there feeling safe once again, one of my classmates got up and started to project her drama on me for one last time. I sat there and took it; after all it was her problem not mine. I had done nothing to this person to cause her barrage of insults. When she finished, the staff turned to me and asked what I thought about what I had just heard. I answered with my usual response, "Nothing." I didn't think anything of what she said. Well, wrong answer, that wasn't good enough anymore.

The head chief told me to stand up and she began to dress me down, right there in front of the whole class. She dressed me up and she dressed me down, she exposed all of my deepest darkest pathologies and fears. I could say nothing; I could only hear her words. I remember her saying, "The buck stops here and this is where the rubber meets the road." I immediately checked out, I completely left the building. Even though my body was there, I was no longer present. It was too embarrassing and too painful to be present in my body; her words were like arrows piercing my flesh. I knew I was crying, because I could feel the warmth of my tears streaming down my face— an unconscious reaction; but I could not hear all of what was being said. I could see her face through my curtain of tears and the seriousness of what she was saying to me showed through her expression and the animation of her body. I would check in from time to time to see if it was safe to return to my body, but NO—it wasn't, it seemed like this ordeal would go on forever and ever. Alas the barrage came to a halt and someone came and helped me to sit down. All I could do was sit and cry, shake and tremble; I was completely devastated. I didn't remember all that was said to me, I only know that I went home from that session and cried for a week. I could not even speak. I held up in my room and didn't interact with anyone for that entire week.

Once I was able to process what had happened to me I felt like I had experienced "Timeless Moments" and I was able to examine the stories I had been telling myself all of my life. I cried and rolled on the floor of my room as I came face to face with the filters that had been created by the stories I'd told myself all of my life. I could see people and places from my past that had helped me share and support these untrue, unsubstantiated stories that I'd been living my life through. I came face to face with the truth about the many people I had hurt and had no clue about the damage I had done. My speech came back through writing first, I had to dismantle the monuments of stories and destroy the filters that had been created in my life. I was given this poem and it poured through me. I wrote it in one sitting.

TIMELESS MOMENT

Words spoken, but not heard, like seeds
falling on barren land,
never to take root, they fell on sand.

Phrases spoken ever so cold; alas these phrases
won't ever take hold,
never to be nurtured, never fed,
never watered, they were just said.
I let them pass over my head, under my feet,
pass through my mind just not too deep.
Snatching from my heart, my feeling of serenity,
my feeling of peace
my joyful feelings, just to say the least.
As they skimmed the surface of my mind
seeking and searching for what it might find.
Nothing was available, nothing was there,
no response, no—not even a care.
Floating in eternity, standing at this space,
Timeless Moment, breathless pace.

Shock waves hitting the senses, while still disconnected,
still out of place, heart beating
fiercely running at a new pace.
Angry and hurt, confused and dazed
wondering what happened so much in my head. Standing
in my majesty, head held high in grace,

be still spoke my soul, be still and listen.
Hold on to the pearls, hold on as she shares,
all else will fall away like rain and glisten
like the tears that you bear.
Floating in eternity, standing in my fear,
Timeless Moment, of what I hold dear.

I can hear the new words over the mind chatter;
they are stern and supportive, yet it does not matter.
The circuit has been broken, the spark burns low
my body stands lifeless with nowhere to go.
On and on the message is sent, requesting,
inviting, cajoling, and teaching
yet I am motionless as I am thinking—
she's preaching. The questions go out searching,
seeking, still no reply on goes the beseeching
as I stand there and cry.
I hear with my ears and listen with my heart
only God knows why my world has fallen apart.
Floating in eternity, standing in my shame,
Timeless Moment, I'll never be the same.

If only I had time, if only I could breathe,
open my heart to feel and to feed
Feed from God's love, and feel the warmth of
his arms enfolding me
now in the midst of this storm.
Congruency of humiliating disgrace, feeling debased
despair like an arrow piercing thin air.
It was totally unacceptable, it could not penetrate my
mind her words were like poison spewing across time.
Speaking her own drama, being her own fan
emanating from her own soul's plan.
Yet the plan and the drama was mine,
the soul's plan was my own
she was a mirror reflecting it straight back to my soul.
Floating in eternity, standing in my breath,
Timeless Moment, I'll never forget.

I had to essentially cleanse my channels of communication, to find a way to open up all avenues and connect to my Higher Self (the God-like nature that exists within every person). This was necessary so I could receive all messages of inspiration so they would be crystal clear, free of any distortion or misinterpretation. My work had begun. I had stopped creating the stories and began to dismantle the old stories that had been running in my head..

DON'T QUIT FIVE FEET FROM THE GOAL/GOLD

We all have dreams and desires. Some we are able to fulfill with little or no effort. Then there are those dreams that take perseverance, digging deep and staying the course. You may have even quit or given up on some of those dreams for various reasons. You may feel you're too old, too weak, not good enough, don't have the money or support. No matter what the reason for quitting, the bottom line is that when you quit and you may have been just three feet from your goal. The three feet I am speaking of could be literal or figurative, the point is that you shouldn't be willing to quit on yourself too soon.

Let me share a story I read many years ago that helped me to understand what the concept of quitting or giving up on my dreams and goals could mean to me.

In the book Think and Grow Rich, *the great author Napoleon Hill tells a story about a man named R.U. Darby, and his uncle who staked a claim, started digging and after much hard work they found a vein of gold. They covered up the vein and went to raise money for the equipment to mine it. They returned to the mine to make their fortune. The man and his uncle worked the vein until the ore ran out; it just disappeared. They kept digging but they never found any more ore. They made just enough money to pay back their investors and then they sold all of his equipment to a junk dealer for a few hundred dollars.*

Now, the junk dealer was no dummy. He hired a mining engineer who checked the mine and calculated that just three feet from where Darby and his uncle had stopped was a huge vein of ore. The junk man went on to make millions from the mine.

My views on quitting drastically changed after reading that particular lesson in Think and Grow Rich. R.U Darby certainly learned from his experience of quitting too soon. He used what he learned to become a very successful businessman. Darby learned that you must persevere through difficulties and not to be afraid to call in an expert when needed.

When you are willing to move out of the way and trust your Higher Self to lead you and to bring all of your good to you, standing firm becomes easier. When you are feeling low, not knowing who your are or who you are supposed to be, that's when the old programs run and you can slip back in to your default behavior. You must be willing to let go of the stories, clear your filters and create a new story. You have the ability to create your life anew every minute of every day. No more fear, no more distorted pictures in your mind and no more cloudy filters. You have to dig deep, no excuses, no justifications, and no tries—just do. Keep moving forward doing a little bit every day towards you dream. DON'T QUIT, keep your eyes on your goal and off of your past, keep putting one foot in front of the other. Forward motion is the key. Stop worrying about how it's going to happen or how it's going to unfold or who is going to bring it or do it for you. Just know that the Universe has got you, it will happen, prepare yourself for the WOW!

6

JOURNALING: YOUR MASTER TOOL

*J*ournaling is one of the best tools you can use to aid in the growth of the human spirit. Some people learn to journal when they are children and continue the habit right through adulthood. Little girls often get a diary as a gift from their mom or dad to write down their moments of joy, intervals of sadness and their little secrets. If the little girl is diligent she will have volumes by the time she finishes high school or goes off to college. Others don't pick up a journal or diary until they find themselves confused or lost in some emotional undertow created by the life decisions they've made.

When you find your way to a journal it can and will open up a world that has been inside of you all the time but you could not see it because it was within. Journaling allows you to separate your thoughts and differentiate them from each other. Journaling opens you up to the world within, connecting you to the many different compartments filled with all of the stories that you created; stories that may or may not be true. Journaling gives you access to the information that is sometimes inaccessible because it's intertwined with all of the other stuff that's rolling around in your mind. The process of free-flow journaling will allow you to bypass your conscious mind and tap directly into the parts of your mind that have been blocked or off-limits to you during your highly emotional times. When you are going through tough times or are perhaps just confused, misdirected or lost in life, journaling can bring great clarity and set you on a road of self discovery.

BENEFITS OF JOURNALS

It may not be an easy task for you at first if you have not been one who journals, but stick with it; the results will be more than worth it. I call journaling a master tool because of all the tools that are in a coach's arsenal, I know that journaling provides the most benefits. Some of the most important benefits of journaling are:

Focus and Mental Clarity: The first thing you will notice once you start journaling is that you see the world differently. Your days become brighter; you may notice things that you hadn't before, such as a flower blooming at the foot of your porch, a butterfly flickering just overhead or a squirrel scampering across your lawn. Your ability to make a decision will become easier and quicker too because the fog is gone from your mind. You'll experience mental clarity at a level that you haven't had in years. Your whole world will come into focus in a way that you have not understood. You will begin to appreciate the little things and become aware of all the things that make up the great Universe that you are a part of.

Time and Space: Journaling will help you to understand your past. You will be able to look back and see the patterns of negativity that you keep falling into. You will be able to understand how and why you continue to self-abuse and self-sabotage. Journaling will allow you to live more fully in the present by slowing you down to smell the roses. You will be able to feel the sun on your face because you know you are truly alive now. You will be able to enjoy each moment as it comes and find things to appreciate and be grateful for today. Journal writing gives you a chance to peek into your future and not only see it the way you desire, but to be able to shape your future in your own way. Journaling is well worth every bit of your effort and will open doors to new and exciting worlds, and you'll gladly walk through those doors once you've recognized them.

Discover Hidden Emotions: You will get in touch with hidden or unknown emotions through journaling. Emotions that you were completely unaware of will come to the surface and you will be able to see and understand those emotions and how they have been affecting your life. Through journaling you will be able to clarify your value system and have a more honest connection to your value system. Journaling will help you to differentiate which values are truly yours and which ones you simply accepted through family, experience or by someone telling you. Your own characteristics will begin to crystalize through the journaling process.

Your emotions are really only your feelings and your feelings are the first way the Universe communicates with you. Becoming aware of your emotions and really paying attention is important; they are often an early indicator of something going wrong. As you learn to understand your emotions you will reconnect to your heart center and truly get in touch with the things that really have meaning in your life.

See Clearly To Set Goals: This process will help you see your path and to tell the truth to yourself first and then to everyone else by doing what you learned through your journal writing. You will be able to not only set your goals, you will be able to set goals that you can actually reach because you are no longer lying to yourself. You will take action based on the clear dreams and desires that are evident to you because of your journal writing. The process of goal setting can be overwhelming, especially if it's not something you normally do. Not every step is going to be easy because goals that are worth pursuing are never easy, but journaling can and will support you in whatever the pursuit. There are many different types of goal setting tools that you can use to help you set goals and they are really helpful. Journaling will help you define and decide what goals you want to aim toward. Once you have been through the journaling process and identified the goals that are important then the goal setting tools can be used to organize the actual goal. Setting a goal and following through will become like child's play because you will be able to see your goal, absent of all of the mumbo jumbo of the 50,000 to 70,000 other thoughts that pass through your head each day. Journaling prior to setting your goals will give you the chance to articulate them clearly and makes their achievement appear closer and more obtainable.

Problem Solving: On any given day you are faced with a multitude of problems; some you solve automatically while others can cause you great stress and woe. Your journal writing can be used as a tool to help you to focus on problems, determine the best way to dissect them and to use your highest level of reasoning to ensure that the best solution is used. It doesn't matter what the problem is, put it down on paper so you can see it outside of the cluster of thoughts that drift around in your mind. Journaling clarifies the many different aspects of the problem so you can analyze it and take the necessary steps to solve it. You will find that personal issues will no longer stump you and your personal relationship issues will not be so daunting. Your interaction with others on all levels will become easy and effortless. Your ability to negotiate and come to consensus in groups will happen almost automatically because journaling will help you train your mind to separate your thoughts quicker and your thinking process will become sharper. Journaling is one of the best tools you can use to improve the skill of problem solving and you can do it alone and in your own time.

Insight and Intuition: As a side benefit of mental clarity your ability to see beyond what is before you heightens, you step into the metaphysics of life. You begin to see things that you would have missed before because you're essentially having a dialog with yourself. You begin to ask and answer the hard questions, such as "why?" or "why not?" or "what?" You also become more intuitive. Because of your heightened awareness of self you are able to listen and connect to your Higher Self. Your ability to empathize, sympathize and walk in the other person's shoes will become second nature because you have met your Higher Self. You are so much more relaxed and available to yourself and for yourself. You will be able to sort through your experiences and be intentional about your interpretation. This ability is only available to people who have taken the time to connect to who they truly are through the process of journal writing. Being aware and in touch with your emotions allows you to be connected to your feelings, which is the first and highest level of communication from the Universe. You will feel at one with all things as you will have a knowing that says all things are possible because you are at one with the Universe. This is all made possible because of the master tool of journaling.

Overall Personal Development: Personal development can't help but occur once you begin to operate from the spiritual level of intuition. Your whole moral compass will be reset as you develop and grow from a spiritual baseline. Your life can and will more than likely take on a new direction. You will feel more in control of your life even though life happens fast and you can feel that you are missing the step by step developments. Journaling on a regular basis will help you to see clearly the processes that are taking place in your world and the world around you. You will have the ability to create and enjoy moment by moment the kind of life you desire. You can't help but grow when you are using the tool of journaling; personal development is an outgrowth of this process. When you look back on a major misstep you see it before you and know without a doubt that you won't make that unhealthy choice again. Your growth comes without you even noticing it until one day you look back and you are not the same person you used to be, you have blossomed into a brand new you.

Estherism: Life Doesn't Happen To You But Through You

> *I often hear people complaining about all the bad things that are happening in their life or how they are experiencing such bad luck all of the time. One of life's biggest inaccuracies is that it just happens; that we have no control over what occurs in our lives. Life doesn't happen to you but through you.*

Record Sufficient Lessons: As you write in your journal you will record important events. You will become more intentional about how you live and the way you pursue your dreams. You will become more conscious of the small things, the simple pleasures of life. You'll be awakened to the experiences and will always be able to relive them through your record created by journaling. You want to remember the events in your life that were good and to have a record of what you experienced, what you learned and what you did to make it happen. The events that turned out wrong or bad will also be recorded for you, to look at what errors you made, how you could do it differently or how to never repeat it again. Journaling becomes a permanent record of your life that allows you to look back and be reminded of your past success and your past failures. A journal is not merely a repository for the lessons you've learned. Your journals become your life story that include all of the ups and downs, ins and outs, wins and losses that you have recorded and it really doesn't matter, it is still your story. You'll have a recording to study and learn many of life's lessons. Journaling can become a documentation of the all-inclusive history of the sufficient lessons you have learned throughout your life, and only you can record it. In these lessons you will find the stories that will inspire you and encourage you to grow and reach for greater heights. You will also inspire and encourage others to move forward just as you have.

Track Your Progress: Last but not least, one of the most important aspects of journaling is that it allows us to track our progress. Journal writing allows you to see how much you've changed over the years and you can see the lessons you have learned as well as the ones you had to go back to school on. You can see the booby-traps and pitfalls that you sidestepped as well as the many victories and triumphs you had along the way. You can see where you made mistakes and where you turned those mistakes into experiences because you learned from the mistakes. Once you take the time to learn from a mistake, it no longer is a mistake, it becomes another experience along your life path. You can look back through the many volumes of your life and see where you have come from and where you are going. Journaling allows you to revisit the developments that have unfolded in your life and the horrors that you escaped. Life happens so quickly that you can miss a whole segment or some details of an important milestone in your life. With journaling you can see the process as it unfolded step by step and the next thing you know the future you had so carefully planned out has arrived.

These are only a few of the many benefits that are derived from the process of journaling. There are over a hundred reasons why journaling is such a powerful tool. Whether you journal for physical or mental health reasons, personal growth, achieving your goal, searching for a new career or repairing personal relationships, journaling will get you there if you're willing to commit. But you must first get started. Start slowly and write a few sentences and begin to build on what you get out of them. Like any habit you must do it and do it often; consistency is the key to becoming a master of journaling. Becoming a master at journaling will greatly increase the quality of your life and will improve your personal relationship with your Higher Self. You will know that the quality of your questions will determine the quality of your answers and that through journaling you'll have the confidence to ask the hard questions knowing that you will find the answers within yourself.

BREATH IS LIFE - ANOTHER GREAT TOOL

When we exhale used air, we get rid of the old and when we inhale new air we reconnect to our spirit. Through the process of breathing we are actually opening a way to purify our spirit. Breath work is a spiritual technology for purification and awakening. If you want to continue to develop and grow and you want to attain true spiritual development, you must get rid of what is worn out or old, such as old beliefs and old thoughts by releasing them through the breath. Breathing is the essence of life; without it nothing lives. Breath can bring life back to the body, a situation, a project or a relationship. Without breath we cease to live, it is our very spirit, the essence of who we are, and when you work with the breath at any level you develop your spiritual skills.

When you find yourself in a situation of anger or you're upset with someone or about something; the quickest way to find your way back to balance and serenity is to breathe. If you can stop and take three deep breaths by bringing the breath from deep within your diaphragm while inhaling through your nose, holding it for about thirty seconds, and then releasing it with a hard blowing sound through the mouth, this will help you to reconnect to your spirit. Breath is life and when you use it properly it can be your salvation. Whenever you get upset, if you stop and take notice of your breath, you will find that it has become very shallow. We tend to hold our breath unconsciously because of the angry energy coursing through our body. This is why it is so important to stop and take note of your breath at these moments in your life. The breath can bring you back to a place of harmony, to a place of joy and to a place of peace. Through the breath you can bring the body back into hemostasis; with the breath you can settle your stomach, clear a headache, calm your nerves, bring your blood pressure down and open your heart. The breath is used in exercise, meditation, and yoga to uplift you, center you, and ground you in your very being.

Breathing is one of the key tools used during the coaching process, especially when a client has uncovered a long forgotten memory or a painful experience. It is also used to help you relax and move out of your way during a session when you want to go deeper into your own past to recover long forgotten issues. The breath is the gateway into the seemly impassable places in the mind and spirit. By using the proper breathing technique you can get past the places deep within your soul that are so dark and painful that you literally lose your breath just thinking about them. When using the breath as a tool during a coaching session, the coach supports you and uses the breath to get you through these difficult discoveries. BREATH IS LIFE.

7

STAYING FOCUSED

 elf appreciation is the valuing and loving of oneself. The dictionary defines appreciation as follows:

1. Gratitude; thankful recognition: *They showed their appreciation by giving him a gold watch.*

2. The act of estimating the qualities of things and giving them their proper value.

3. Clear perception or recognition, especially of aesthetic quality: *a course in art appreciation.*

4. An increase or rise in the value of property, goods, etc.

5. Critical notice; evaluation; opinion, as of a situation, person, etc.

6. A critique or written evaluation, especially when favorable.

This is a pretty comprehensive definition of appreciation and it covers the type of appreciation I am talking about here.

Appreciation of oneself doesn't seem to be as big a problem for men as it is for women. Women often get so busy in their day-to-day lives, especially if they have a family with small children; they often forget to take care of themselves. They forget what it feels like to be appreciated by someone else because they are so busy taking care of and appreciating everyone else. They are the cooks, maids, carpool drivers, nannies, nurse-aids, housecleaners, wives and lovers. They often wear so many different hats that they could easily develop multiple personality disorder and not even know it. On the other hand, a man seldom has to take on all of the different roles, especially if he is married and is the chief breadwinner. Yet there are times when the roles are reversed and men step up to take on the many jobs that are traditionally carried out by women.

I had one such client; I'll call him Stephen to protect his privacy. Here is Stephen's story:

Stephen is a well-educated father who decided to switch careers after many years and several jobs at executive level in the corporate world. His wife, also an executive, chose to continue her climb up the corporate ladder and agreed to support Stephen as he embarked on his new journey to find himself. Stephen decided to go back to school to get licensed in the healing art of massage therapy because that's what he felt was calling his soul. After completing his schooling he obtained his license and began to slowly work his way into the field of massage work. After a few months Stephen felt he wasn't having enough success at massage work, so he decided to take on some contract work in his old line of business and work from home. He knew he had to bring in some money to help supplement his wife's income and keep the family afloat. In addition to this he also maintained the household; cooking, cleaning, laundry, chauffeuring the kids, shopping for clothing and food for the family and upholding his husband duties. Any need for research, or special projects that arose within the family, Stephen handled them too.

When we first started our work together, self-appreciation was not on the list of things he wanted to address. He was mostly focused on getting into the field of healing work by getting a solid business plan. He was exhausted and depressed yet he didn't know he was exhausted and depressed. I asked him one simple question, "When was the last time you did something for yourself to have fun?" The question caught him off guard; he had not even entertained the thought of himself and fun at the same time. He couldn't remember or come up with an answer. We moved forward to explore the concept of him carving out some time in his life to do one thing a week that *brought him joy. It was hard at first for him to come up with something, but I insisted that he stick to his goal of finding one activity a week for himself.*

Stephen was so programed to take care of everybody and everything that he forgot himself. He forgot how to appreciate himself. In our exploration we talked about self-love, self-care and self-appreciation and how important it is to practice the concept of self-preservation. He learned that if he didn't take care of himself he really couldn't take care of all the other things at his highest capacity.

He eventually got into a consistent pattern of doing something fun and enjoyable for himself each week; he began to see his worth and to value and love himself. Once he satisfied that part of his heart, focusing became easier. Once he was able to focus he could help me to help him concentrate on the original goal of our partnership of developing a solid plan to cultivate a business for himself and allow him to do what he loved.

So now is a good time to ask yourself these questions. What is it in your life that makes you happy? What is it that brings a smile across your face, makes your heart leap with joy, causes you to feel energized and on purpose when you are doing it? Well, that's your heart song. To find your heart song, you must allow yourself the time to be still and listen to your internal rhythm; the music that is playing in your soul. The messages that are being whispered deep within your heart calling you forward, urging you to stop what you are doing, focus, and pay attention. In order to hear what your heart is saying you must appreciate yourself, know your worth and value yourself for who you are and not for what you do. Love yourself because you are God's greatest miracle and a Divine expression of the Universe. You cannot and will not find the focus necessary to hear your heart song without first appreciating yourself.

HOW TO STAY FOCUSED

Are you living in the past or spinning your wheels and not getting anywhere? Are things in your life out of whack or in complete chaos? Do you find yourself jumping from project to project? Do you find that you keep quitting jobs, relationships and never really completing what you start because you lose interest? Perhaps it's time to refocus on your goals and get your life back on track. Getting focused will help you to learn how to handle disappointments, overcome failures and produce solutions. If you are ready to move forward with your life and get focused again then let's begin with getting organized. I have outlined some steps below that have proven helpful for my clients.

1. KEEP AN ORGANIZED SPACE

✔ Spending ten minutes cleaning your space at the end of the day will help you have a more organized lifestyle.

✔ If you don't need your phone to do your work, put it away for a few hours.

✔ Prioritize regularly; interruptions will happen which will cause you to reprioritize your goals and commitments.

2. MAKE A TO-DO-LIST

✔ Separate your to-do list into three lists: things to do that day, things to do the next day, and things to do by the end of the week.

✔ Put the most important or hardest tasks first. It's better to save the more manageable tasks for the end of the day when you're more tired and less compelled to complete the hardest tasks.

✔ Try to focus on the top three to five items on your list before adding new ones.

✔ Include breaks in your to-do list. You can reward yourself with breaks.

3. MANAGE YOUR TIME

✔ Track your activities for a week or two to see how you're using your time.

✔ Break up more time-consuming tasks with shorter, easier tasks.

✔ Think of the shorter tasks as mini rewards instead of work.

✔ Put a cluttering plan in place rather than waiting until the urge hits you.

4. MAKE TIME FOR BREAKS

✔ You can choose an activity to do during your breaks. You can set a goal to read for thirty minutes over the course of three hours.

✔ Don't sit at your desk all day. Get up during some of your breaks and take a short walk, or walk up a few flights of stairs.

✔ You can even set a timer to go off after every half hour or hour of work, signaling that you should take a break.

5. DON'T REINVENT THE WHEEL

- ✔ Stick with what works. Once you find a system that works, keep using it.

- ✔ Periodically review your processes.

- ✔ Don't use miscellaneous files; use more categories when filing and group things together like utilities, department stores, etc.

- ✔ Choose tools that work. If it becomes inefficient don't hesitate to release it.

These steps will help you get organized and know that you don't have to try to do everything at once. Start out by working with the ones that are easiest for you to implement and then add more once you have mastered the first steps. You may not need to use all of the above steps to get organized so you can just choose the ones that work best for you. These steps will help you to get organized but they will not keep you organized. You will have to continue to prioritize and stay focused on your goals and commitments. Focus is what you're trying to achieve by using the above steps to organize yourself.

SPEAK ONLY WHAT YOU WANT
AND WANT TO SEE

When you decide to focus in on your life and take responsibility for what it will look like and how it will be, that is a major step. It's important to know that at this point you must speak only what you want in your life and only what you want to see materialize in your world. This may sound like an easy task but for many it is not. Thoughts become things, and when you speak them out loud those thoughts take on form and shape much quicker. In the first chapter of the Bible, Genesis, it states, "In the beginning was the word." The word is the most powerful tool you have for creating. It was the word that was used to speak this Universe into existence and it is with the word that we all create our reality. What I am saying is that what we think and focus on will become our reality. Yet when you speak out loud what you are thinking and focusing on, it comes into your reality much quicker.

The principle of thoughts becoming things is immovable. It is absolute. There is no way around it and when you speak those thoughts out into the ether or the Universe you bring about the manifestation of those thoughts much sooner than if you were to keep them on the mental level. When you put your thoughts into words you add more power to those thoughts and super charge them because you are commanding the Universe to bring forth that which you desire. It is no longer just something you are thinking about, you are declaring that thought to be so it must take form.

We don't operate in a vacuum. Every thought goes forth to create with other like thoughts in the Universe. The power we call God or Infinite Intelligence or the Universe is always in operation, it never sleeps. Now you may think, *Well, if everything I think or say must come to pass, what about all of those dreams that have never seen the light of day? If it's that simple and predictable why don't all of the things I think and say come to pass?* Well, we never just want one thing or think one thought. Scientists tell us on any given day we have over 70,000 new thoughts. When we think that many thoughts in a day, there is the great likelihood that some of our thoughts will contradict one another or cancel each other out. Some of those thoughts may even be mutually exclusive too. For example:

One client I worked with had firsthand experience with thoughts and words canceling out each other. I will call her Lena. Lena wanted to become the top producer in her office and in the region. Everyday she thought about being the top producer in her sales office. She told her co-workers that she was going to be the top producer every month, and in so doing, she was speaking this desire out loud. She wanted it with her whole heart and soul so every day she thought about it, visualized it, and spoke it. Lena had gone as far as creating a vision board, and on that vision board were pictures of her in her new corner office, and some of the trips she would win, the car she would buy and some of the upgrades she would make to her house. Lena was speaking her desire to be the top sales person in the region into being. She even visualized herself receiving the honor as the number one producer in the region. But this same person would go home every evening and say to her husband, "Honey, no one at the office knows how good I am or what I have to offer or how much I try." What Lena didn't realize was those kinds of thoughts and words must do what all thoughts do: strive to become part of her reality, even though they were negative. That is what was happening to her. In one of our sessions I shared with her these thoughts; "The person that thinks they are underappreciated often becomes underappreciated", and "If you think you can't, you can't. If you think you've lost, you have." And that's not where she wanted to be if she was going to reach her goal of becoming the top producer in her office or in her region.

To say the least, Lena was facing some periods of doubt in herself and in her ability. When she got home in the evening after a long, hard day of work and expressed those doubts to her husband he would agree with her. She didn't realize that the very thing she wanted so badly was being blocked by her own words so her desire to reach the top was not materializing as fast as she had hoped. In our sessions, we explored all the thought processes she had been entertaining and were able to isolate the negative ones that were cancelling out her higher desires. Lena was able to get back on track by mining her mind and speaking only what she wanted. She discontinued the habit of going home and complaining about her day to her husband, and focused on only what she wanted to materialize in her life. She was able to reach and maintain the goal of top producer in the region and had set even loftier goals. Lena leaned to speak only what she wanted in her life.

That example shows you how easy it is to get caught up in focusing on the negative thoughts and produce just the opposite of what you desire. So now you understand why some of the thoughts you have don't come to pass; because others have gotten in the way or just plain negated them. That is why it is important to speak only what you want. If the person in our example had matched what she was saying and thinking with what she wanted from the beginning consistently, she would have demonstrated her goal much sooner. But she had competing thoughts that canceled each other out and she was completely unaware of her own thought process.

You may say, "What about the things or circumstances that happened in my life that I never even thought about?" Well, when the unexpected lands in your path it is always a stepping stone in a journey to get you to a place you have been thinking about or desiring to go. Say for instance you want to effect a change in your life; you want to go from point A to point B, automatically the Universe sets out to make it happen based on your thoughts, your desires. It doesn't have to be a geographical change. It may be that you just want more money, friends and laughter in your life and less bills, debt and stress. Sometimes for God or the Universe to get you there, you must be drawn through unthought of territory. A lot of things will change and happen along the path of that journey that you never thought about or expected. Your job is to continue to think and speak only what you want until you get what you have asked for. You may not understand everything until later, after you have passed through all of the distraction and arrived at your destination. Your job is not "the how" but to allow the Universe to bring about "the wow".

I lived the first half of my life in the control freak category. I had to know everything about everything so I could be sure that it would all turn out exactly the way I wanted. It seldom did because I was always bemoaning the imaginary pitfalls and living my own self-prophecies. I would speak out loud all of the horrible and negative things that I thought and felt would go wrong – and they did. It was exhausting, it was nerve wrecking and I was always multi-tasking, always trying to stay ahead of the game. I thought I had to make it happen, I had to ensure every step was done precisely the way I envisioned it. I didn't know I was cancelling out my vision with my own words. I did this not only in my life but also in everyone else's life too;

my kid, my partner and friends. What I didn't understand or realize was if I was trying to do it all, where was there any room for the Universe to help me? The Universe will not force its will upon you. It will not interfere or coerce you to accept its help. Since I was running the show, I had to carry the heavy burden of the outcome, whether good or bad, it was all on me. The Universe allowed me to have my way, to get what I was speaking and do what I felt was best although it was not always what I was trying to achieve.

Words are life and they create the situation and things in our reality whether positive or negative. I know you might say, "How can a little thing like words have any effect on what I create in my life? But they do. After all, it was The Word that called forth the light and the life of our world, according to the Bible. It can be difficult to be conscious of every word you speak but that is exactly what you must train yourself to do. I'm saying you must try to speak positively more often than you speak negatively. You must guard your thoughts, mine your mind, and not allow your mind to run amuck. It won't happen over night but gradually it can and will happen if you make the choice to speak only what you want in your life.

8

CREATING YOUR OWN REALITY

As you move through the process of coaching, the reality of self-responsibility becomes very apparent. Hopefully you will begin to understand that you and you alone are in charge of your life and how you show up in the world. This is a huge benefit of Spiritual Life Coaching, to help you understand just how powerful you are and empower you to create your own reality. At some point along your journey you will begin to increase your awareness and educate yourself about the power of the subconscious mind. You will learn to stop, shut everything down, disconnect from the outer world and take some time to pay attention to how your mental focus influences the world around you. You may use the process of meditation, quiet walks in nature or just being still for a short time each day to still your mind. You will become more connected to your true self, that part of you that is aligned with the Divine. Tapping into your true self brings about an awareness that causes you to pay attention to what's showing up in your life. You will recognize on a higher level how and if what is showing up in your life corresponds to your thought process. It may come as a surprise to you just how many of your own personal thoughts have been the seeds that produced your outer reality. This includes those thoughts that are buried deep in your subconscious and you have completely forgotten you even had them, but your unawareness does not negate the affects of those thoughts in your life. It doesn't matter whether or not you are aware of the thought, if it has been accepted by your subconscious mind it will manifest in your material world. That's not to say you cannot cancel a negative thought or remove an unknown program that has been wreaking havoc in your life. The great and wonderful thing about all of this mental stuff is that you are in charge and you have the power to create with your thoughts and to destroy or cancel what you have thought into your reality if it is not to your liking.

All energy and matter at all levels is created by and is subordinate to the Omnipresent Universal Mind. Some call this power the Universal Mind, Intelligent Consciousness or the Subconscious Mind, and even God. It doesn't really matter what you call it as long as you understand that we are all connected through a singular intelligent consciousness and it is all-knowing, all-powerful, all-creative and always present. Your subconscious mind is the gateway to the Universal Mind—this Universal Mind operates like a genie granting your every wish whether you judge that wish to be good or bad—it is granted according to your desire. The subconscious mind does not differentiate based on your judgment of the thought; it just accepts the thought once it penetrates the subconscious mind. Whatever idea you give your attention to will grow; right or wrong, good or bad.

THE UNIVERSAL LAW

Thought is the beginning of all creation. The law of mentalism is the first Universal law which states that everything starts on the mental level. According to the Kyblion's first Principle or Law The All Is Mind, "This Principle embodies the truth that "All is Mind." It explains that THE ALL (which is the Substantial Reality underlying all the outward manifestations and appearances which we know under the terms of "The Material Universe"; the "Phenomena of Life"; "Matter"; "Energy"; and, in short, all that is apparent to our material senses) is SPIRIT which in itself is UNKNOWABLE and UNDEFINABLE, but which may be considered and thought of as A UNIVERSAL, INFINITE, LIVING MIND." "It also explains that all the phenomenal world or universe is simply a Mental Creation of THE ALL, subject to the Laws of Created Things, and that the universe, as a whole, and in its parts or units, has its existence in the Mind of THE ALL, in which Mind we 'live and move and have our being.'"

Therefore everything we see and experience in our physical world begins in the invisible, mental realm. This law tells us that there is a single Universal Consciousness from which all things manifest. The Omnipresent Universal

Mind creates all of the energy and matter at all levels and that is the same mind that is in you. Your mind is part of the Universal Mind and your reality is a manifestation of your mind. This is true Mind Power and it is within you. Everything you see, touch, taste, feel and hear started on the mental level that is within you. This is what the coaching process teaches you, and empowers you while supporting your continued understanding of how this power within you operates.

YOUR THOUGHTS ARE POWERFUL

The subconscious mind always responds to our inner dialogue and self-talk. Furthermore, our subconscious mind uses our beliefs and self-talk to create the experiences in our lives. Our thoughts become things, so it is important to choose the good ones. Like produces like; what you think about will eventually show up in your reality. Our inner beliefs and self-talk may be rooted in limiting beliefs that were formed early in childhood and now they no longer assist us in achieving our goals and dreams. You must be willing to examine every belief, every value and every principle you live by to determine if it's yours. You may discover that they're something you've adopted because that's what your parents or someone else you looked up to believed. You may find that your thoughts are being formed by some other person's influence or someone else's beliefs and truths. Therefore, you're not creating the life you truly want but a life based on false belief. Mine your mind, you may be surprised by what you unearth lurking there that you were completely unaware of but is creating total chaos in your life.

I often share with my clients that wherever you find your behind your mind put it there. Your outer world reflects what you think and believe internally.

Estherism: Your Best Thinking Got You Here

Your Best Thinking Got You Here means that the situation you find yourself in didn't just happen, you didn't just end up in a mess by chance, it was your mind working at its finest. Sometimes your mind works overtime to create the madness you find yourself in, and believe me, it won't be the mind that gets you out of the negative situation.

You can bring about the changes you want by mining your mind; in other words, paying attention to what thoughts you hold in your mind. Know that if you are going to bring about a change in your life you must first connect somewhere deep within your soul at a level that goes beyond believing to the level of knowing. Your desire to succeed, to change your life, must be a burning fire that burns greater than any of your skepticism and fears. This metaphysical quantum shift is the only way you can establish belief in your own mind. You will start to see small victories as you apply this principle, and it's the small victories along your journey that will bolster your spirit and help you get to a place of proficiency at creating your reality.

TODAY'S THOUGHTS WILL BECOME TOMORROW'S REALITY

Let me start with a very important virtue, one that you must have to move forward in knowing your true self. It is integrity. Integrity is a virtue that is necessary to stand in your true self as you travel your path to creating your reality. Different people can interpret the meaning of integrity in many ways. To some it means having a personal set of values and holding to those. To others it means being true to yourself and your upbringing. What does the word integrity mean to you? The questions I am asking are, "Are you being true to yourself? Are you being congruent in how you live your life and how you show up in your life?" What does integrity look like to you? It is important to examine every segment of your life to see and know if you're truly in integrity with yourself. These are significant questions you need to ask yourself. Being out of integrity in one area of your life permeates every part of your life eventually. It erodes the very fiber of your being and destroys your character and self-esteem. When you lie to yourself and to others because you think no one can see you, that lie sticks to you and begins to aggravate you. You are out of integrity. You're pretending to be one way in your public life and living totally differently in private. This is incongruent behavior and you live in the constant fear that your secret will be discovered. Examine your behavior to see if you are showing up in integrity. Sometimes integrity can be as simple as doing the right thing for the right reason, even if nobody knows or notices that you have done it.

Integrity plays a major role along this journey you're on because integrity determines the nature and the quality of your thoughts. The higher the quality of your thoughts, the higher the quality of reality you create. The thoughts that you think today will determine your tomorrow. The average human has 70,000 thoughts per day. Now imagine how many of those thoughts are golden and can be turned into some magnificent project, or maybe a successful business. How about a new home or a new love or more money? All of these treasures are right there in your mind. On the other hand, just imagine how many of these thoughts are just plain useless or negative, and realize the havoc they are creating in your life. You must learn how to differentiate between the positive thoughts and the useless thoughts. Remember, "Thoughts Become Things," so you want to be able to choose the positive thoughts as well as the good ideas that go with the positive thoughts.

I keep coming back to the mind, to drive home the point that the mind is the instrument by which we humans create our reality and our world. I know this is a lot of responsibility to shoulder, but who else is responsible for the things that are happening in your world? If you truly examine your world and stand in integrity it will become very difficult to accuse another person, place or thing for how you have created your world. We all have free-will and can choose what we want at any given moment. We can choose negatively or positively in our lives. If you choose to hold onto the negative thoughts then you will see negativity in the form of poverty, sickness, lack, hatred destruction, suffering, unhappiness and failure. That is the crop that springs from seeds of negative thinking. If you choose to dwell on positive thoughts the majority of the time then the crop of those seeds will be success, happiness, abundance, health, joy, prosperity, and love.

By becoming conscious of your thoughts you implement new habits. Sometimes this can be a daunting task, particularly since all day long you are just going on your merry way without even thinking about what your thoughts are. Then you must also take into account the hidden beliefs of your past, beliefs that you don't even know you have anymore – beliefs that are responsible for generating their own nearly invisible thoughts. WOW! Where do you begin? How can you get the task of mining your mind started? Just do what you can. Your life is already filled with challenges and the unexpected no matter what you do. It's not always easy. We all go through tough times when we wish we could just quit that job or end that relationship, or not get out of bed that day. Days when we wish we could walk away from everything and never look back, but most of the time we don't. Why don't we walk away? Because we know that no matter how challenging certain situations can be, the reward or the upside is greater so we stick it out. We know that if we at least do what we can things will get better, they always do. But sticking it out should not be enough for you when you could have it your way. The same is true when it comes to working with your thoughts; you just do it, you do what you can and you will start to experience such pleasure.

WHAT'S YOUR PLEASURE?

Whatever your dreams, desires and hopes
They're never beyond the Universal scope
If you can see it, hold it in your mind
and believe it with your soul
The Universe will deliver riches, fame, and wealth untold

WHAT'S YOUR PLEASURE? –
It's yours beyond the greatest measure

Keep your heart open, keep your mind sharp
Stay present, stay in the moment, that's how it all starts If
you can believe it your mind can weave it
and you will achieve it
The Universe will mold, shape and construct
your bold mentality

WHAT'S YOUR PLEASURE? –
You can have it all in worldly treasure

Create what you will, the Universe must always yield
You're the designer, the architect and the gold miner
You're the selector, the pattern maker and the director
Just take hold of that Infinite
all-encompassing powerful role

WHAT'S YOUR PLEASURE? –
You can have it all at your own leisure

Step into mastery, be the captain,
make things happen even faster
The power is yours to keep, whether awake
or in a deep sleep
It's yours forever, it's never lost, it's your birthright
paid for at great cost
Accept the greatness of higher altitude and
embrace the magnitude of your reign

WHAT'S YOUR PLEASURE? –
It's always delivered without any
discrepancy or displeasure

Ask what you will, ask what you want—
the Universe must fulfill
Choose your own destiny and create your new world
with laser clarity
With all of the skill, knowledge and grace
you create at your own pace

*The world that you desire, the way you aspire
is yours to acquire*

WHAT'S YOUR PLEASURE? –
It's more treasure than you could ever, ever measure

GRATITUDE

Gratitude is the fuel that makes it all work. Just like you must put gas in your car before you can operate it, being in a state of gratefulness lubricates the wheels of the cosmos to bring your reality into existence. Being grateful is a disposition of the Soul; it is an attitude, a way of being. When you take on the state of gratitude you open up a channel of abundance from the Universe and there is nothing you can't create. Each day upon rising, take on an attitude of gratitude and watch how smooth and prosperous your days become. Gratitude brings about a chemical change in the body that can and will produce a feeling of peace, a state of healing and a sense of euphoria. The Universe will unfold and release your heart's desire when you are grateful. When you are grateful you cannot help being unpretentious and humble, and in your humility you will find your strength. There is no truer statement than that one, because when you can stand in your humility you are at your most powerful true self; you have completely surrendered to the Universe and that's when the real miracles happen.

One of the simplest things most people miss is the everyday miracles they experience. Maybe we miss them because we have such high and lofty ideas about what a miracle should look like. The first thing we must learn to do is to recognize our blessings no matter how big or small before we can honor them. Blessings show up in many forms. They can be as simple as a smile from a person passing you in the street, or as large as being healed from what you've been told was an incurable disease.

Once you learn to recognize and be grateful for the blessings that show up, more can and will start to flow into your lives. Whenever you put your attention to something then it starts to multiply. The more you show gratitude for your blessings the more blessings will show up in your life. I say don't take them for granted, and what I mean is, don't just assume that they are going to happen because you are special or because you and you alone are entitled. This is not about entitlement - and I don't mean to say that you are not special because we are all special to the Universe. What I know is that it is our Divine right to be joyous, prosperous and live abundantly. We are all children of the Universe and are entitled to all the good there is in the Universe; it is there for the asking. That doesn't mean that you have to do anything for the Universe to bless you, but it does mean that you have to be something, and that something is grateful.

I can attest to how gratitude works because I have experienced the effect of it in my life. I have been blessed and abundance has flowed throughout my life, and the more I acknowledge and appreciate the blessings of the Universe, the more they are multiplied in my life. Even during the low points of my life when it appeared that I didn't have anything or anyone to turn to I remained grateful. When all doors were closed and I didn't even have a nickel, somehow someone would show up and show out with a blessing. The right people would always come into my life at the right time to further my cause and help fulfill whatever desire or need was present. I learned to surrender my desire and my will to the Universe and to have faith that I would be guided to what to do, be or say. I learned that you can't beat the Universe giving, no matter how you try, and you can figure out the how of the Universe. So as long as I am grateful, the blessings continue to flow in my life with great abundance.

9

LIVING YOUR MOST
AUTHENTIC LIFE

n chapter eight I talked a little about the virtue of integrity and how important it is on your path of knowing yourself. Integrity, like most words, can and has been interpreted in many ways to fit the individual's need at the time. Integrity is one of those words that gets dropped in leadership and personal development circles, particularly when you get into the discussion of values. But integrity is a virtue that must be fully explored by you and embraced according to your own beliefs and understanding. Being honest and truthful is the basic meaning of integrity. Keeping your word and standing in your own truth is another layer of integrity. Having an uncompromising and predictably consistent commitment to honor moral, ethical, spiritual and artistic values is another layer of integrity. You can even go into another layer by having strong moral uprightness, moral principles and knowing and holding to your value system. Integrity is the inner sense of wholeness stemming from living your life according to qualities such as honesty, decency, trustworthiness and consistency of character. What's important here is what integrity means to you. What does integrity look like to you? It is important to examine every phase of your life to know if you have defined and truly understood integrity. Are you in integrity with yourself?

Estherism: Are You In Integrity

When I ask the question, "Are you in integrity?" I am asking other questions as well. "Are you being true to yourself? Are you being congruent in how you live your life and how you show up in your life?" The very thing you think you are hiding is what everyone sees. In your mind you actually believe that you are showing up in integrity because it appears so in your mind. NOT!! People may not be able to put their finger on it or articulate it, but they know something is off about you; they sense the inconsistency in you that you think you've hidden. So, ask yourself, "Am I living in integrity with my true self?" I hope we can all answer with a resounding yes!

How do you have integrity and what does it look like when you're in integrity with yourself? As an individual you must honor your word, and commit only to what you can and will do. Don't make promises you can't keep, and if you do, let the person or the people it will impact know that you can't keep your promise. Be willing to stand in your truth, and if that truth changes, embrace the change and stand firm in your new truth. In other words, be willing to own your own stuff; take responsibility for the things you do and say regardless of how painful or shameful it is to you. Here are some examples of owning your own stuff:

You tell your friends that you want to start your own business and quit the dead-end job you go to every day. In reality you have no intention of leaving, you don't have the courage, the strength or any kind of plan to leave that dead-end job. You are out of integrity with yourself.

You have a service business, such as doing hair. You overbook your appointments just in case of cancellation and you end up getting behind because no one cancels. You say "sorry" to the people you keep waiting, but you can't help feeling that in-the-moment twinge of guilt. You are out of integrity with yourself.

Suppose you are having a sale on your skin care products and you tell your customer that they need to buy a lot more different products because the way to get the best results is that they must be used together. You know you are not telling the truth but you want to boost your sales for that week so you oversell that customer. Some people would call this plain lying or cheating, but that's what integrity is about - being honest. Being honest with your customer and yourself.

This is a favorite of mine and I have been guilty of this one so many times. You promised yourself to eat healthily and get to the gym at least three times this week. But it's been a bad week, and when Monday rolls around you're off and running on the same routine. Satisfying that late-night sugar craving in the evening gives only a transitory sense of contentment before the self-loathing voices remind you that you are out of integrity again.

All of these examples are about behavior and dishonesty with self. When you lie to yourself and to others because you think no one can see you, you are out of integrity. It is easy to tell yourself that you are not hurting anyone and that it only affects you. Or you may think that it's just the way things are and everybody does it so "no harm, no foul". You're pretending to be one way in your public life and living totally differently in private. This is incongruent behavior and you live in the constant fear that your secret will be discovered. Examine your behavior to see if you are showing up in integrity. Sometimes integrity can be as simple as doing the right thing for the right reason even if nobody knows or notices that you have done it.

Business leaders who shamelessly enrich themselves at the expense of their customers, stockholders, and employees are out of integrity and it reflects poorly on their industries. The cost of this dishonesty and lack of integrity is passed on to the ones who can least afford it. Judges who take bribes and teachers who sexually abuse their students give us a reason to pause and disappoint us greatly. They too are out of integrity and set very bad examples in our society. Yet many turn the other cheek and pretend that it has nothing to do with them, so they do nothing. That behavior only serves to support the lack of integrity in life on a grander scale. When you are out of integrity it doesn't just hurt you but those around you who interact or do business with you.

What you will find when you stay in integrity with yourself is that life goes better; you'll feel better about yourself and your relationships will be better. Integrity is a description that is earned, and one that should be prized. If you have it, guard and nurture it. If you don't yet have it, pursue it zealously. It's certainly worth the change in behavior you will have to make to earn it.

WHEN YOU LIE TO YOURSELVES, THEN WHAT?

In the early seventies I was a consultant for Mary Kay. "Fake it 'til you make it" was one of her most famous sayings and it stuck with me. What Mary Kay was saying to us was to pretend in our minds that we were successful until we became successful. She taught us to visualize our success as we worked on the physical level to make it happen. It was not a lie even though we had not yet arrived at the desired level of success; the phrase kept the vision alive while we worked toward our goal daily. There is a difference between a lie and an inspirational phrase. An inspirational phrase is used to help you believe and keep you focused on your goals. A lie is just a lie.

When you lie to yourself it's really hard to move forward, or to facilitate any kind of change in your life. When you lie to yourself you only fool yourself. Deep within your soul you know it's a lie, yet sometimes you're so disconnected from your innermost self you can't tell the difference between the truth and the lies you've told yourself.

We all know people who perpetrate a fraud or put on airs and pretenses, but they know it and eventually as you get to know them—they get real with you. You can see through the façade and they no longer need to lie to you or themselves; they feel safe enough to be themselves. But that's not always the case. The problem comes in when a person doesn't realize they are lying to themselves and they keep up the pretense. They buy into their own hype and ignore the callings deep within their souls. From time to time they may feel a little twinge or a yearning deep within but refuse to acknowledge or investigate what it is or what it means. What then? What happens when you lie to yourself? Stagnation—no growth—no movement along life's path. You continue to live an inauthentic life.

When you tell a lie, sometimes it immediately causes harm to someone else, or it could allow something to happen for you that otherwise wouldn't have. Maybe the lie opened or closed some doors for someone, or prevented some harm that possibly would have happened. All of those things can and will happen on the physical level or conscious level. But what is that lie doing on the subconscious level? When you lie, if you are not a sociopath, there are certain emotions that present with the lie, i.e. guilt, shame or sorrow. Even if you are able to hide these emotions they still occur within you. You may be able to ignore them at the immediate time and put them out of your conscious mind but—HOLD ON! The lie sits in the subconscious, out of sight and out of mind and it sticks to you through the emotions that it conjures up, doing even more damage in your life. The negative emotions on the mental and spiritual level are what cause disease on the physical level. Guilt, shame, fear; all of these negative emotions will show up on the physical level in the form of hypertension, cancer, heart disease and diabetes. The lies affect the sociopath's life too. They don't feel the emotions attached to the lies, but it doesn't negate the effects of the lies on the physical level.

You don't have to imagine the chaos that is created in your life when you lie to others and yourself. I'm sure you can just look around you and you will see acquaintances, friends and even family members whose lives reflect the results of deceit. When you lie, life can become so perplexing and confusing until you and no one else will really know who you are. If you don't know who you really are anymore then how can you expect anyone else to know? The world you create is out of touch with reality and with what your authentic life path is meant to be. Can you really say what's next when you are living a lie and refusing to acknowledge the fantasy you have created? No. So let's ponder this question; "When you lie to yourself, then what?" Think about how or if this question shows up in your life.

YOU CAN'T GIVE WHAT YOU DON'T HAVE

If you've ever taken a flight, you have heard this instruction given by the flight attendant; "If you have a small child with you, put on your mask first and then put on the child's oxygen mask." What the flight attendant is saying is make sure you have oxygen before you try to help someone else. This is similar to what I am talking about here; you can't give what you don't have. You can't help anybody if you can't help yourself.

This is especially true for women, but some men find themselves in this predicament too.

I have encountered individuals who want to be all they can be for everyone else. They make huge sacrifices for their spouse, families, churches and communities. They are always available to do one more errand or to take on one more project. They have a hard time saying no or refusing to assist someone. They're always there to give a hand, a kind word or a strong back and at the end of the day they have nothing left for themselves. Then they get up the next day and do it all over again, never stopping to replenish their own spirits or to re-energize their own body and soul. One day they can't get up or out of bed because they're tired, weak, and worn. Their health is failing and they need to seek medical help for several physical conditions in their body. They can't bear to get up to face another day. Their minds have shut down, they feel dejected, disoriented or just plain old used up. They're depressed, empty and broken inside. They think this just all of a sudden happened to them; they woke up and everything was shot. But nothing could be further from the truth. This is what happens when you keep trying to give what you don't have and do not take care of yourself.

You think that you can and that you must solve all of the world's issues or at least all of your family problems. You can fix everything even if that everything is not yours to fix. You try to fix it anyhow. You don't even realize that you don't have it to give and you don't even realize that you don't always have to have it to give. You try and eventually you cry. The key is to first acknowledge that you don't have it to give. The way for you to acknowledge that is by stopping, getting still, and listening to your spirit. Begin by doing only the things that will replenish you.

This is an important step on your path to creating your most authentic life. You must not only acknowledge your need to pull back and relish yourself but you must also take deliberate action. Take steps by doing things that are restorative and healing to you. Take some time, nourish yourself and rethink how you want to give and what you want to give to others. Make sure that your emotional storehouse is full before you begin giving your time and energy to others.

WHAT I KNOW

I know what I know and what I know, I know
I know that I know God and that God knows me, I know
that he loves me because he lets me be I know what I know
I know that the sun will rise and it will shine on its own
each day because that is what it does, from early morn
until the early dawn I know what I know
I know that I am alive and I know that I have survived,
and that again I will thrive I know what I know
I know that I have loved and that I am loved from people
below and God above I know what I know
I know that I am blessed with family and friends, some
friends for a season but family will be there for all the right
reasons I know what I know
I know that I have a purpose and that any day it will
surface from deep within to bring me the win
I know what I know
I know that I am gifted with talents from beyond and with
these gifts people shall be lifted I know what I know
I know that I will transform, transcend and transmute,
and by Grace I will re-assimilate to a better person,
a higher race I know what I know
I will leave this plane someday, my work shall be done, I

*will go to a higher plane because my race will have been
run I know what I know and what I know, I know*

DEVELOPING AND LIVING YOUR VISION

Now that you're standing in your integrity, you've learned to give only from your overflow and to stand in your truth, the next step is to develop and live your vision. Prior to you moving forward there is a key step you must do before you can accomplish any goal, vow or resolution. You must first make a decision to have a vision. Have you asked yourself, "Where do I want to be in five years? In ten years?" Steven Covey wrote, "All things are created twice." First there is the mental creation and then the physical creation. The vision is the first creation; mentally we must see it before we can manifest it in the physical. Once you make the decision you can then tap into the creative resources of your psyche and begin to describe and develop your vision for your new life. It's not always easy but it is necessary and doable. Take the time to visualize where and how you see yourself in your new life and what you want to accomplish. *Have you thought about where you want to be five years from now? How about three years or even a year from now? Many people don't even know where they will be in six months from now.* Without a vision you have no idea where you're headed because your vision is your life map and with this vision you will shape your life and all of your future endeavors.

If losing weight is a part of your new life, see yourself at your ideal weight; get pictures and images of what you want to look like. Be willing to cut your food intake in half and watch what you put into your body and when you put it in. Become conscious of the amount of exercise and movement you have in your life. Be willing and determined to increase your exercise at intervals that will support your efforts. If a new house is a part of your new life, begin visualizing what the house looks like inside and out. Start to see each room, see the colors on the walls of each room, the light fixtures, every closet, the floors and every detail of the house. Visualize yourself in your new home, walking through it. See everything about it right down to the tiniest detail, and use your visualization to bring it forth. Then take care of your business as much as you can and get all of your ducks in a row by ensuring that your credit is on point and that you have some savings for your down payment. Do some research into the many loan options and find the one that works for you. Start packing, and pack up all of the things you are not using or don't need on a daily basis. By doing this you're letting the Universe know that you're ready to make that move. If it's a car, go down to the dealership, sit in the car you want, smell it and immerse yourself in the feeling of driving that car. Then test-drive it. As you're driving in your old car each day, imagine yourself in the new car. As you look upon the dashboard, see it as the new car's dashboard. Visualize and see yourself in your mind's eye in that car. Get pictures of the car and put them in a place you can see every day. It doesn't matter if it is a Volkswagen or a Bentley, whatever your vision is the Universe will grant it once you make a decision to bring that vision into your new life.

Our brains don't know the difference between reality and fantasy, so you can dream as big as you can believe. If you can believe in your vision just fifty-one percent, you will achieve it. Whatever you imagine yourself to be you will become. When you visualize your subconscious mind goes in high gear to make it happen and whatever you hold in your mind will manifest in your world. Visualizing is the language that speaks directly to your subconscious mind. Once the vision takes root in the subconscious mind it's just a matter of time before it shows up in your material world. By visualizing what your success is you become the co-creator of your own success along with the Universe. It doesn't matter what your dreams and desires for success may be just make sure that your vision matches it. You must be committed and consistent with your visualization process. You can't do it for a few days and when you don't see any results, quit. You must be willing to hold that vision until it manifests in your life. It could take a week, a month or years. The key is to hold your vision until you get the desired results.

Let me close out this chapter by saying there are many different types of program, books, and workshops you can use to implement your vision, but ultimately the work must be done by you. You cannot have more success than you can see for yourself. Although your coach is there to help you choose the plan that will best work for you, it is your vision, it is your plan and your coach will support you as you embark on your most authentic life.

10

CONCLUSION—IT'S NOT THE END, IT'S ONLY THE BEGINNING

GET ACQUAINTED WITH SELF

o help you meet the real you on this journey of self-discovery these are some of the questions you will need to ask. Do you really know yourself, inside and out or do you just think you do? What makes you happy? What stimulates you? What stirs your heart? What brings you to tears? What makes you sad? These are some of the questions that you will explore at the beginning of your journey. You may not be able to answer these questions honestly and completely just yet, but along the way the answers will become very clear. It's a good idea to take time to check in with these questions as you move along your path.

Here are more questions you can ask yourself that will also help find a starting point.

- How important is it to you to be loved and to love?

- How would other people describe you?

- Do you really care how others think about you?

- How do you want to show up in this life/world?

- How important are your victories?

- How much does peace mean to you?

- What are you willing to sacrifice to achieve your goals?

- Describe one key event in your life that you feel shaped who you are today?

- What motivates and inspires you?

- How do you experience the Universe or God?/ Or Do you?

- What do you feel is your life's purpose?

- What is it you hope to accomplish professionally and/or personally from the coaching experience?

So put your dreams in front of you. Look for words, symbols or signs that will support you and you can associate with your reason for embarking on this soulful journey that will leave you forever changed.

Spend some time alone answering these questions this is where journaling really comes into to play. You may even want to spend some time each morning in quiet solitude to contemplate about who you are and what you know and believe about yourself. You are worth getting to know and in order to do that you are going to have to embrace yourself, by loving yourself just the way you are now. Don't wait until you think you have arrived, you can love who you are right now, yet still move foreword on your path of discovery. You don't have to be perfect first to love yourself. Really I don't believe that anyone is perfect because when you reach perfection you no longer have a reason to be here on earth. So find a way to love who your are including all of your little imperfection, own them, celebrate them and know that the imperfection are the reason for your being here to learn and grow.

I include the golden rule, "Do unto other as you would have them do unto," here because I believe it is so necessary to remember and incorporate this into your life. Treat those around you with the same love and respect that you would want to be treated with. Don't gossip, lie or be deceitful to those around you, or to anyone; these behaviors come back and bite you. Life is like a garden and your word are the seeds for creating and manifesting; so whatever you plant with your words, that's the crop you will get. You can't plant carrots and expect roses. Think before you speak, everything that pops into your head does not have to come out of your mouth. First, ask yourself is what I'm about to say kind? It is true? Is it necessary? Does it improve upon the silence? If you can answer yes to all four questions, then your words will resonate with authenticity and love.

SELF-COMMITMENT

What are you willing to commit to in order to accomplish you dreams? Ok let's dust off our dreams and get started with the rest of our lives. Over time we are programed to dream less and look at things more realistically. We are conditioned to settle or accept what we believe is our lot in life. We have been programed and conditioned to give up all together and completely forget our dreams. You tell yourself you have to make a living, you have to be responsible for taking care of your family and paying the bills, there's no time for visualizing, no time for fantasizing and chasing pipe dreams, you have to make it happen. How wrong you are, without dreaming, imagining, and visualizing you are lost, anyone without a vision begins to slowly die.

Why Vision? Vision is the beginning point for leading the journey. Vision is what keeps you focuses and inspired. Vision is your alarm clock in the morning it gets you started on your way each day. Vision is your caffeine in the evening it keeps you going to finish the one last task before bed. Vision touches the heart, stirs the mind and motivates the spirit. It becomes the criterion against which all behavior is measured and a catalyst for all dreams to be realized. You can create the reality that you want if you have a clear vision. You can create the reality that you want if you have a clear vision. There are three steps to bringing your vision to life. First on the mental level the vision is crystalized, you must see it before we can create it. Then emotionally you must feel it and embrace the emotions of how you will feel once you have what you see in your mind? The physical level is the finial step and is the material level on which your vision comes into being.

Have you taken the time to think about where you want to be 5 years from now? How about 3 years or even a year from now? Many people don't even know where they will be in six months from now. Without a vision it is virtually impossible to know where you're headed, because your vision is your road map. Be aware that vision always refers to a future state or condition that does not presently exist. And with this vision you will shape and create your future. You can determine what you will and will not do based on a clear vision. Vision gives you a sense of control, direction, and destiny. When you have a vision of where you are going or what you want to create; you have a sense of control over what's going to happen each day in your life. Your inner compass is in full operation so your direction is on point and you will be able to see your path clearly. Once you've casted that vision you will feel confident that your destiny is just within reach and can be fulfilled in this lifetime. Casting, or drawing out your vision from the heart and diligently working to carry it out, requires character, integrity, and truthfulness. All of these values are within you just call them forth and commit to live your most authentic life.

HOW

How do I know when I have arrived?
When I've arrived at that place of peace
How do I know when I hear?
When I hear that still small voice speak for my release
How do I know when I see?
When I see all that life has to show me about my past
How do I know when I taste?
When I taste the fruit of the spirit of my soul
How do I know when I have touched?
When I've touched my essence and who I am unfolds

How can it be that I am so unsure?
So unsure of where I am to be with thee
How can it be that I am so blind?
Blind to the understanding of all that I see
How can it be that I am so hungry?
Hungry for the knowledge flowing all around me
How can it be that I do not feel?
Feel all of the warmth of love that grows in my heart
How can it be that it is so quiet?
Quiet in the depth of my soul because we are apart

How will I ever reach that comfort?
Comfort of knowing that I am safe in His arms
How will I ever learn to listen?
Listen to the still small voice that sounds the alarm
How will I ever fulfill my promise?
My promise that was made before time was
How will I ever be conscious?
Be conscious of moment by moment just because
How will I ever notice the unseen?
Notice the unseen that is around me all abuzz

How is really not the issue nor is it important, I know the answers to all of the how's.

How is a three-letter word—a question that opens up the mind to a multitude of possibilities and opens up the soul to a New Beginning.

YOUR PATH

Every experience is an opportunity. Every mistake is an experience, if you choose to learn from it. We are at choice every moment of our lives. We can choose how we react to any situation. If you decide to look at an action or step as a series of mistakes than you will never begin., you will learn by doing. Walk through your fear, the very things that you're most afraid are the things you must be willing to face head on. It may feel uncomfortable for you to move ahead, you may feel like you are going off half-cocked and ill prepared, but that is why your coach is there.

Walk while you cry and know challenges will come but they also will go, it is all about your reaction. You will have some incredible highs on this journey but you will also experience some very low days that will make you want to give up or at least cry, but this is when you must be able to keep going to walk while you cry. Keep putting one foot in front of the other and know that these times will come but that you are just one good cry away from fulfilling your dream.

Failure is not fatal it is just another stepping-stone to success. So when I say there are no mistakes just experiences, I want to break it down even further. Without mistakes no learning takes place and without any learning there is no growth. Growth is one of the main components to creating the successful life you want. So if there is no growth your dreams and desires will eventually fail: either your life will become rigid or stagnate, but in either case you fail to adapt to changing conditions in you environment. I want you to clearly get the message here – mistakes are merely experiences and people, however, only learn and grow by making mistakes.

Mistakes are only Experiences

In every adversity there is an opportunity to grow and to achieve something even greater. If you see every mistake as an error, or as your inadequacy then you will miss the seeds within it. Every misstep, blunder or slip-up is just an experience and holds seeds of wisdom within for you to learn and grow from. Without mistakes there is no chance for learning to take place. Without any learning, there is no growth."

Knowing and accepting that you can make a mistake and keep going is how you will continue to grow until you reach the pinnacle of success. A mistake is not failure and it doesn't mean that you are not capable of recovering from a mishap in your life. You sometimes have to try many different approaches to a problem before it's solved. Or you may have to take several paths before you arrive at your destination, but it doesn't mean you've failed. So if you are not getting the results you want the first time or even the fifth time keep going until you do.. And remember mistakes are not a bad thing they are just the inefficiencies in your system that allow you to learn and grow.

DON'T! I repeat don't beat yourself up, remember what we focus on expands and what we ignore diminishes, so if you focus on yesterdays failures then that's what you will get more failure. If you sit in judgment of yourself, fill your head with negative talk all day then that is what your day will be filled with negativity. There will be times when you become so wrapped up in working hard, doing it right, staying engaged and reaching your goals that you push away the very joy and prosperity that you are trying to attract. You can become so impatient and screw up when trying to set, focus, and accomplish your goals that you forget to go easy on yourself, but be light and graceful about reaching your goals and creating abundance. Stop allowing that self-defeating voice to have a platform in your head; don't let negativity rent space in your head either. And finally discontinue the self-sabotaging behavior that comes from self-doubt and beating up on yourself. In spite of all the mistakes you make, each and every day you get 24 new hours to get closer to victory and create a new reality. And if you think that only a chosen few are meant to be glorious, successful and celebrated, think again. You owe it to yourself to realize that as you travel this journey you always have choices to make that will determine how high your soar. Sometimes our finest hour is not birthed on a bed of roses but on a bed of nails and by overcoming mistake by turning them into experiences and realizing the lessons and growth from each one you can soar.

STAY THE COURSE

Not quitting is the first step to ensure success. You will have setbacks; you will stumble and fall but pick yourself up and begin again right where you are. You will have some good days and some bad days just remember that you have the power within to create your future. You will never fail until you quit. Just take that first step and get started, you will get better with each step you take and each new insight you have. We have been given supernatural strength to overcome. One of the strongest forces in this world is the human spirit and our will to succeed. In the face of adversity many will quit but don't give up. Never, never give up, never abandoned your dreams. Tell yourself quitting is not an option and adopt this way of thinking about everything in your life. You must know and believe that the only failure is failure to get up and try again. Greatness is revealed most when a person has beaten the odds, and gotten back up after dodging all the jabs, hooks and uppercuts that life can throw at them. Failure is never final but quitting is -- SO DON'T

FINALLY KEEP MOVING

There will be days that everything seems impossible, you are stuck in traffic, you're already late for your next appointment, your tire blows and your phone is dead. This is when you have to say to yourself, just **"keep moving"**, repeat it over and over in your head until your situation changes. Even when you've taken time to plan everything just right, you've sent the invitation, made the calls inviting everyone to your event and only a few show up. Your check is short because of some unforeseen hiccup in payroll and you think what else can go wrong, **"keep moving"** repeat it over and over because you will open yourself up to making something happen. Keep moving repeated over and over will allow your mind to be creative and come up solutions. Even if your best friend doesn't show up to your event and she promise to come and bring guest; you missed passing an important certification test that is needed for your next promotion by 1 point and have to wait for six months to take it again; and the new employee that you thought was going to be dynamite quits **"keep moving."** When everyone in your family thanks your crazy and you'll never succeed, and you are no where near where you want to be financially; you've worked you buns off and still success hasn't come yet, just **"keep moving"**. Those that have gone before you never quit, they kept moving until they succeeded and you will too. Ninety nine point nine percent of the time you will get where you're going but you must keep moving, because if you stop you are guaranteed to not get there and failure is imminent. **SO KEEP MOVING** onward and upward, focused and forward to your own level of victory and success.

Where do you want to go, what do you want to do and who do you want to be? Only you can answer these questions.

Enjoy the journey the destination will appear. Congratulations, your journey has just begun!!!

The Beginning